PRIVATE OWNERS
on the CAMBRIAN

Mike Lloyd

Welsh Railways Research Circle

Acknowledgements

Over the years a large number of people have contributed information which has assisted me greatly in the preparation of this account. I apologise if I have omitted anyone from the list below.

In particular, I would like to record my thanks to Bernard Holland for providing me with a list of Cambrian area private owner wagons built by the Birmingham Railway Carriage & Wagon Co., and for much useful information on the wagons of the collieries of North Staffordshire. He also took on the onerous task of reading through this account suggesting additions and corrections. Other people who contributed are S Bell, Gerald Davies, C C Green, Harry Leadbetter, the late J Lumley, R Miller, H Morgan, N Owen, the late Mrs M Pugh, D Rees, the late John Stratton, J P Richards, L Tavender and Tudor Watkins.

The following public bodies also rendered assistance -

Bersham Heritage Centre, Hereford Public Library, National Library of Wales, Shropshire Record & Research Centre.

Lastly, but by no means least, I would like to thank my wife Irene who has typed and patiently amended this account several times as fresh information or corrections have come to hand.

Mike Lloyd

The Welsh Railways Research Circle

The Welsh Railways Research Circle brings together modellers and researchers who specialise in the railways of Wales and the Border Counties. The principal purpose of the WRRC is to put members in touch with others of similar interests and to go some way to avoid duplication of research effort.

In addition to the publication of books, the Circle publishes a twice-yearly journal, 'The Welsh Railways Archive', and a quarterly Newsletter for its members.

Full details of the Circle's activities and a Prospectus may be obtained from the address noted below.

ISBN 0 9527267 1 8

British Library Cataloguing-in-Publication Data.
A catalogue record for this book is available from the British Library.

Edited and designed by Tony Miller, Great Gidding.

Printed in Great Britain by Stylaprint, Elton, Cambridgeshire.

Published by The Welsh Railways Research Circle
22 Pentre Poeth Road
Bassaleg
Newport
South Wales,
NP1 9LL.

PRIVATE OWNERS on the CAMBRIAN

Contents

Abbreviations used in this Book

Birmingham RC&W Co.	Birmingham Railway Carriage & Wagon Co.
Gloucester RC&W Co.	Gloucester Railway Carriage & Wagon Co.
Midland RC&W Co.	Midland Railway Carriage & Wagon Co.
MRC	Model Railway Constructor
MRN	Model Railway News
RCH	Railway Clearing House
RM	Railway Modeller

References

Fuller details of publications annotated with a reference number ([n]) can be found in the bibliography on page 52.

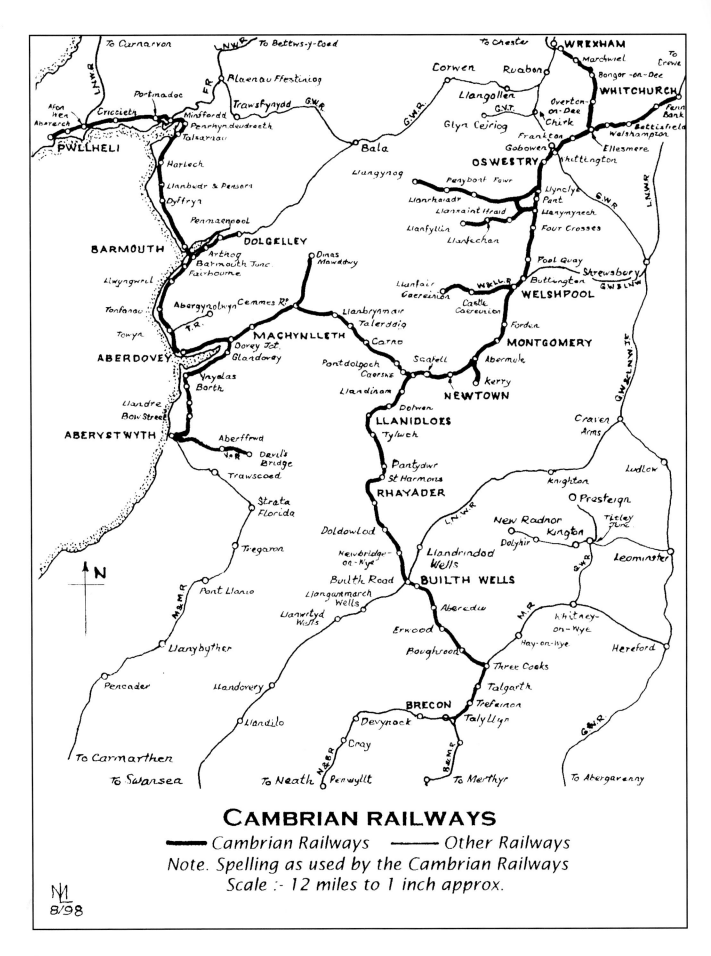

CAMBRIAN RAILWAYS

━━━━ *Cambrian Railways* ──── *Other Railways*

Note. Spelling as used by the Cambrian Railways

Scale :- 12 miles to 1 inch approx.

iv

Introduction

About fifteen years ago the Cambrian Railways Modelling Circle Newsletter published an article that I had written on private owner wagons on the Cambrian, which aroused some interest and produced some correspondence in subsequent issues. In an unguarded moment, at a WRRC AGM some five years ago, I was pounced upon by the Hon. Editor of the Circle's journal and asked to submit a revised article.

While I must admit to not having worked industriously on it during the intervening years, I have occasionally blown the dust off the file to add or revise information. Thus it transpires that the amount of information that I have gradually amassed is far too great to feature in *The Welsh Railways Archive*, the Circle's journal, and now forms the basis of this book.

Due to the length of time since these wagons were commonplace, and to the disappearance of much of the associated information, no study can be described as definitive. By offering the fruits of my research in this manner, however, readers may come forth with more information to help fill the inevitable gaps.

After some brief notes on the sources used for my research and on the regulation of privately-owned wagons by the Railway Clearing House, the bulk of the book is an illustrated directory of private owner wagons to be seen on the Cambrian.

For simplicity the directory will be in two sections; the first will deal with wagons operated by traders domiciled on the Cambrian system, the second with those off the system.

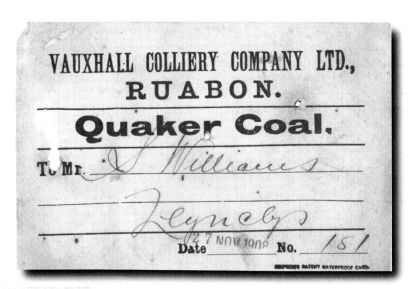

Two wagon labels from Ruabon companies, both routed to Llynclys.

See pages 42, 44 & 45

Chapter 1

Sources of Information

Railway Clearing House Publications

Sources of information were many, one of the most important being two books issued by the Railway Clearing House in January 1926 and October 1933. These two books listed private owners who were parties to the Commuted Annual Payment Arrangement. The 1926 book covered the empty haulage of PO wagons. Whilst outside the Cambrian period, it seems worth recording that wagons operating under the 1926 agreement carried 'C.C.' plates, while those covered by the 1933 agreement (introduced 1st July 1933) carried a five point yellow star, six inches in diameter, either painted or on a plate above the painted wagon number.

Telephone Directories

Thirty-five years ago there was still a large number of coal merchants and other traders still in existence and listed in the telephone directories.

It was, therefore, a simple matter to work through the two RCH books to extract merchants on the old Cambrian system and to contact those listed in the telephone directories by letter. A large number of those firms had their origins in the early days of this century, or earlier, being passed from father to son. Results varied; quite often nothing - not even a reply - but sometimes a photograph would arrive plus, once or twice, reminiscences which went beyond the coal business.

Trade Directories

Another helpful source was trade directories but these need to be treated with caution. Although a merchant is listed in the directory it does not necessarily indicate that he, or she, was a wagon owner or hirer. Their coal may have been delivered in a colliery wagon or one belonging to an agent. Where they do prove their worth is in indicating the period during which a firm was in existence. Some firms had a very short life; for example, Ernest Shepherd of Oswestry appears in that town's directory for 1900 only.

Wagon Builder Records

An equally important source of information was provided by Bernard Holland in the form of a list of private owners who purchased or hired wagons from the Birmingham Railway Carriage & Wagon Co. almost from the inception of the Cambrian Railways until 1912. Unfortunately the Gloucester Railway Carriage & Wagon Co., whose photographs are preserved in the Gloucester Record Office, built for very few wagon owners on the Cambrian.

Wagon Measurements

In a few cases I was actually able to measure private owner wagons including one with dumb buffers dating probably from the 1860/70s.

Some Cambrian area PO wagon drawings and photographs have been published in the press and, where appropriate, I have given references.

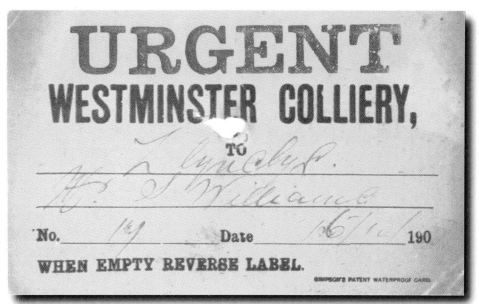

Wagon label from Westminster Colliery, Wrexham.

See page 45

Overview of Traders

Probably the biggest private owner on the Cambrian was the Porthywaen Lime Co. but, as their largest customers were in the Midlands, the loads travelled only short distances over the Cambrian, to Oswestry or Buttington Junction, so most of the haulage revenue went to the GWR or LNWR. The Pwllheli Granite Co. also had a large number of wagons and here the Cambrian did better, provided, of course, that the wagons were not routed via Afon Wen.

Prior to the coming of the railways into Mid and North Wales coal was very expensive and beyond the means of working people, except in areas served by the Montgomeryshire Canal or perhaps seaports.

The poorer sections of the community used wood, peat if available locally, or culm if living on the coast. In 1858, before the coming of the railway, seventeen coal merchants and dealers in Newtown were listed in Slater's North and South Directory.

Three firms listed are colliery companies, namely Brymbo Coal, Ruabon Coal and Westminster Coal. It is interesting to speculate as to whether they owned their own barges on the canal. Rather confusingly they all had the same agent, Ed. Davies Jun., at the canal basin.

In the same directory Llanidloes and Machynlleth are shown to have two coal merchants each. On comparing the Newtown entries of 1858 with those of 1889, the names have changed completely and the merchants were now situated at the 'Railway Wharf'.

From the few surviving records and pictorial evidence, most coal on the Cambrian was obtained from the North Wales and Staffordshire coalfields, although a record of wagons received at Doldowlod in 1916/18 compiled by the late John Stratton suggests that owners on the Mid-Wales line obtained a large proportion of their supplies from South Wales. Anthracite would, of course, have come from South Wales.

Whereas volumes have been written on railway companies and their wagons there is a dearth of information on private owners with the exception of a few large companies. I have tried to rectify this in regard to private owners on the Cambrian but many records have been destroyed in the last few decades so at best it is fragmentary.

Use of the Traders' Directories

Where there is information on the firm or its wagons this has been included in the relevant directory. To date I have been unable to find any private owner on the Cambrian who operated tank wagons. However, by 1922 the Anglo-American Oil Co. Ltd. and Shell Mex Ltd. were located at Cambrian Wharf, Oswestry.

Although I have limited my research mostly to the Cambrian era many firms lasted into the GW period and in a few instances into BR.

Lastly a word on the drawings. In only a few cases have I been able to use dimensions from a wagon by measurement, a general arrangement drawing, or given on photographs such as those of the Gloucester RC&W Co. Any such dimensions are given on the drawing.

Where no measurements are known a length of 15ft 0in external has been used as this was quite a common size at the beginning of this century. In these cases no dimensions are given on the drawing.

Livery is a difficult problem when working from photographs. Black and red tend to look the same on photographs taken 90 to 100 years ago due to the emulsion used on the plates. On drawings based only on photographic evidence, I have given my interpretations of the livery.

From W. Y. CRAIG & SONS, Ltd.,

BRYNKINALT COLLIERIES

CHIRK, NORTH WALES.

To **PORTHYWAEN** (Cam. Rlys.)

For Messrs. PORTHYWAEN LIME Coy.

Slack.   Wagon No. 366

Date 2 4/8/ 190 8   When Empty, Home.

This Wagon must be unloaded within 48 hours after arrival, or demurrage will be charged at the rate of 3s. per day.

L. W.—207

Wagon label from W Y Craig and Sons, Brynkinalt Collieries.

See page 34

Chapter 2

Railway Clearing House Specifications

Firstly, some notes about the involvement of the Railway Clearing House with the design and registration of privately owned wagons.

In 1887 the Railway Clearing House (RCH) produced specifications for 8 and 10 ton private-owner coal wagons to which all wagons built after that date had to conform. The specifications were updated in 1899 but only for 10 ton wagons.

There was another revision in 1903 which made provision for 10, 12, 15, 20 and 30 ton wagons. In 1907 yet another specification covering 8, 10, and 12 ton wagons was introduced.

Before a wagon was allowed to run over the country's railway system it had to be inspected by an official of the railway on which its home was situated. To verify the inspector's approval a plate was fixed to the solebar usually, but not always, towards the left hand end. *(Figure 1)*

Not all privately-owned wagons which were based on the Cambrian were registered by that company. Quite often a coal merchant hired wagons, perhaps from a wagon builder. In this case the wagon would probably have been registered by the railway company in whose territory the wagon builder was situated.

Such an example is the 8T wagon of Edward Davies of Machynlleth which was registered by the GWR. The wagon was built by the Gloucester RC&W Co., which is situated on the GW - MR Gloucester Docks branch, and was presumably on hire to Edward Davies. In contrast, the Joseph Williams and Sons Ltd. wagon was registered by the Cambrian as it was owned by Joseph Williams and based on that railway.

The Demise of Dumb Buffers

In 1889 the RCH announced that no newly-built dumb-buffered wagons would be registered by the railways. At that time an overwhelming number of PO wagons were dumb-buffered, so 1910 was set as the year when such wagons would no longer be allowed to run on main line railways. The date was later extended to 1914.

It was clearly uneconomic to replace all the dumb-buffered wagons by new sprung-buffered ones. The wagons were therefore converted by the replacement of the headstock and the fitting of self-contained sprung buffers. When converted, a wagon had again to be approved by a railway inspector and a plate bearing the word 'converted' was affixed to each side. *(Figure 2)*

This was not always straightforward. When a wagon was in such a state of disrepair that it required two new solebars or one new solebar and three cross timbers, the wagon had to be reconstructed, but if the ironwork, wheels etc. complied with the latest RCH specification they could be re-used.

In the case of a dumb-buffer wagon the standard buffing and drawgear had to be adopted. A reconstructed wagon had to be checked by a railway inspector and, if passed, subsequently carried a diamond shaped plate, similar to the 'Converted' plate but bearing the word 'Reconstructed'.

Plate 1 - Steetley Co. Ltd.

A close up view of the buffer on the far side of the wagon shown in Plate 9 - a Harrison and Camm Type 5A buffer. See Figure 3 opposite.

M Lloyd collection

Conversion of Wooden-buffer to self-contained Spring-buffer Wagons

Early in 1900 a spring buffer was evolved which contained in one unit a buffer-ram, a volute spring, a guide and a plate to which the buffer-guide was fixed. This buffer was secured as a complete unit to the headstock by two strap-bolts and two bolts.

The RCH approved this design of a self-contained buffer and issued the following instruction for frame alterations when fitting:

a. Shortening and tenoning of solebars;
b. Fixing of the necessary iron parts;
c. Fitting of new headstocks to which the buffers were bolted;
d. Incorporation of continuous draw-gear by the fitting of two long drawbars, one of which to be fitted with a volute spring, stop and washer, the two drawbars to be connected by an 18in cradle.

As well as being economical, such a conversion had the added advantages of not weakening the longitudes and diagonals by the shaping necessary to accommodate a laminated buffer spring nor being affected by the varying wagon frame widths between solebars.

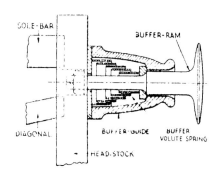

Notes from
Railway Wagon and Tank Construction

*Additional drawings of buffers are held
in the WRRC Archives.*

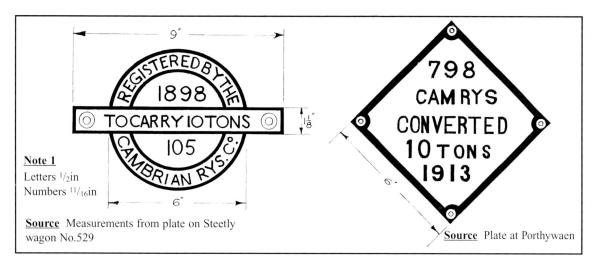

Note 1
Letters ¹/₂in
Numbers ¹¹/₁₆in

Source Measurements from plate on Steetly wagon No.529

Source Plate at Porthywaen

Figures 1 & 2

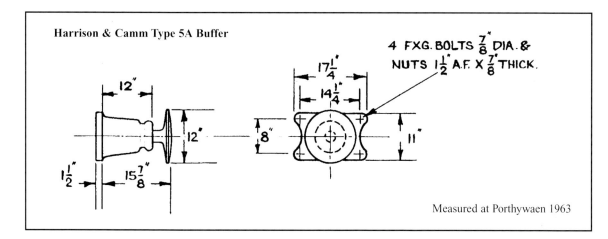

Harrison & Camm Type 5A Buffer

Measured at Porthywaen 1963

Figure 3

Chapter 3

Directory of Traders based on the Cambrian

ABERDOVEY

Evan Davies

Wagon No.4 leased from Birmingham RC&W Co. between January 1912 and January 1914.

Griffith Davies & Son

5 Glan Dovey Terrace, Aberdovey. Listed at January 1926.

Lewis Lewis

Wagon No.1 purchased 1879.

ABERYSTWYTH

J B Balcombe *(Plate 2)*

Wagon(s) built by the Gloucester RC&W Co. but not likely to have run under the name of Balcombe for long since he appears to have been connected with the mine for only a short time, 1870/1. Their further history is not known.

Drg: MRN May 1960.

George Green

George Green came to Aberystwyth in 1848 and by 1856 was the manager of the Cambrian Foundry, which he later owned. The firm made much of the machinery for the local lead mines and when these began to close the firm looked abroad for its markets.

The foundry was situated opposite the goods yard but was burnt down in 1908.

Wagon No.1 purchased from Birmingham RC&W Co. in 1876.

John Jenkin-Jones

Two 10T wagons Nos.10 and 11 were bought from Birmingham RC&W Co. in March 1895. They measured 14ft 6in x 7ft 0in x 3ft 9in internally with steel underframes. The firm was still in existence in 1926.

Peter Jones *(Plate 3)*

Peter Jones was a local entrepreneur born in Aberystwyth in 1847 and, besides being a coal merchant, had interests in slate and lead mining. He retired from being a coal merchant in 1914. The firm also had a depot at Bow Street station.

Wagon No.1 was built by Gloucester RC&W Co. This was an 8T, 5-plank open, tare 4-4-0 with dumb buffers, slightly raised ends and wooden brake shoes on one side only. Small lettering on the side read 'To be forwarded to W.W.Powell, White Rose Station, B & M Railway'.

Lisburn Mines Co. Ltd.

This firm may be a cuckoo in the nest! Although the addresses are given as London and Aberystwith *(sic)* the mines it operated were to the south east of the latter around Pontrhydygroes and would have been better served by Trawscoed or Strata Florida on the M & M R.

Wagon No.3 was purchased in 1872 from Birmingham RC&W Co.

Charles Meehan & Son *(Plate 4)*

A long-established Aberystwyth firm with offices outside the goods yard. The firm had a number of wagons, the highest number seen on a wagon is 24

Plate 2 - J B Balcombe, Aberystwyth

In the early days of the Cambrian Railways, lead ore was an important traffic although the industry was then in decline. The big mines were situated at Dylife and Van. The Van mine appears to have used ordinary low sided open wagons, and the only photograph located showing a wagon specially built for lead ore is this one built for J B Balcombe; how the ore was loaded and unloaded is a mystery. Note the padlocks.

The board on the side gives the following internal dimensions: length 12ft 6in, width 6ft 9in, depth at side 10in, depth at centre 23in. It seems probable that the wagon(s) were used to transport ore from Llandre, to where it would have been brought by cart or pack horse.

Courtesy Gloucester RC&W Co.

but that is not to say that there were 24 wagons running at any one time. Two styles of wording have been noted, 'Charles Meehan & Son' and 'Meehan' see *The Cambrian Railways Vol.2* [5] for the latter. The wagon bodies are believed to have been painted green with corner plates, strapping and running gear perhaps black. Lettering was white.

Henry E Taylor

Wagons Nos.1, 2 and others purchased 1869-70 from Birmingham RC&W Co.

Thomas & Jones *(Plate 5)*

Coal, lime and general merchants, still in existence in 1933. Wagon No.2, a 6-plank open with a steel channel underframe and single-sided brake, was built by the Midland RC&W Co. The ends were slightly higher than the sides and curved down to meet them.

William Thomas

Wagons Nos.1 and 2 purchased from Birmingham RC&W Co. in 1874.

Plate 3 - Peter Jones, Aberystwyth

Built Gloucester RC&W Co. The livery is possibly chocolate (see Broughton & Plas Power Colliery wagon for comment on page 34) or perhaps red-oxide with white lettering. Ironwork appears to be black.

The small lettering reads 'To be forwarded to W.W............(name not readable)/ White Rose Station, B & M Railway'.

Courtesy Gloucester RC&W Co.

Plate 4 - Charles Meehan & Son, Aberystwyth

Part of a photograph showing four wagons which have been just repainted and lettered. Note painted-over 'MERCHANTS' on fourth plank down on first wagon.

At first glance this wagon appears to have an unusual lettering style but closer examination shows that it is due to the sign-writer making allowance for the strapping. Livery is believed to have been a dark green although a simpler style of lettering seems to have been adopted in the 1920/30s, as noted in the text.

Courtesy R W Miller

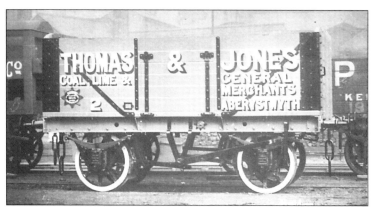

Plate 5 - Thomas & Jones, Aberystwyth

Built by the Midland RC&W Co. and note the steel channel underframe. The livery was probably medium grey, white lettering with black shading and black ironwork.

Courtesy C C Green

BARMOUTH

John Lewis _(Plate 6)_

An old railwayman stated that this was a short-lived concern, coming into being probably in the 1930s.

BUILTH WELLS

Thomas Lant

This concern probably came into existence shortly before World War I. Peter Matthews has recorded two examples of the firm's wagons. One was a 10T 5-plank 16ft 6in long open with a side door and is numbered 229. The other was a long low-sided all-steel wagon built by the Cambrian Works in 1925. This only ran in the Lant livery for a short period as Thomas Lant was merged with other companies into the British Quarrying Co. Ltd.

Drg: MRN Jan 1965 - steel wagon.

British Quarrying Company Ltd. _(Plate 7)_

B.Q.C. (as its wagons were lettered) was formed by merging six quarry companies, viz: J Arnold and Sons, Ceiriog Granite Co., Clee Hill Dhu Stone Co. Ltd., Thomas Lant and Field & Mackay Ltd.

Wagons were painted red-oxide, lettering white shaded black. After nationalisation these wagons were not taken into stock and NON-POOL in white letters on a black background was painted on the left of the top plank.

Drg: MRN Jun 1949.

Photos: MRC Nov 1956, RM Oct 1955.

Plate 6 - John Lewis, Barmouth

Reputed to have been a short-lived concern; livery possibly red oxide, white lettering, shaded black.

M Lloyd collection

DINAS MAWDDWY

Mawddwy Coal and Lime Co.

The title of this firm is frequently prefaced by 'Dinas' but a letter-heading of 1871 confirms the title as shown. The company was almost certainly owned by Sir Edmund Buckley, chairman of the Mawddwy Railway and local entrepreneur, who lived in the mansion 'Plas Dinas' at Dinas Mawddwy. In 1871 the firm's office was at the Mallwyd station, the manager being Henry Worrall who was also manager of the Mawddwy Railway.

In 1867 twelve wagons numbered 12-23 were hired from the Birmingham RC&W Co. but were returned by 1869. Part of a wagon belonging to the company may be seen in photograph 3716 by the L&GRP. The same photograph appears on page 49 of the _The Mawddwy Railway_.[33] The company was still in existence in 1926.

DUFFRYN

Morris Griffiths Williams

Wagon No.1 hired for the period September 1882-November 1890. Wagon No.2 purchased October 1883, both wagons built by Birmingham RC&W Co.

ELLESMERE

W & W Nunnerley _(Figure 4)_

A Walter Nunnerley is listed in the directory for 1855 as corn merchant and by 1891 he is listed as a Corn & Coal Merchant in the station yard at Ellesmere. By 1922 he is not mentioned as a corn merchant but is still listed in the 1926 RCH Handbook.

FOUR CROSSES

John Davies Rogers

Wagon No.1 hired August 1885-October 1889 from Birmingham RC&W Co.

LLANBEDR & PENSARN

Robert Richards

Seven wagons hired 1882-1914, namely Nos.2, 4, 5, 6, 7, 8 and 53 (ex No.3) from Birmingham RC&W Co.

C C Green, in _Coast Lines of the Cambrian Railways_ [3], makes reference to a wagon belonging to Richard Bros. of Pensarn being destroyed in a mishap at Penmaenpool in 1919. One R Richard of Llanbedr & Pensarn received a shipment of lime in a Porthywaen Lime Co. wagon No.54 in 1899.

Was it the same firm?

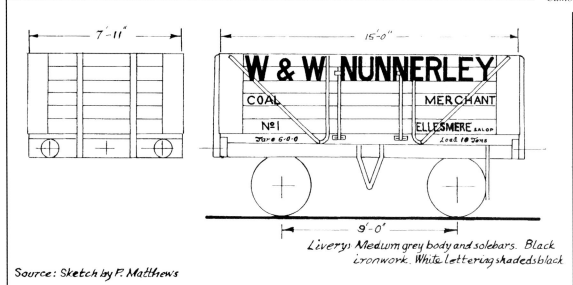

Livery: Medium grey body and solebars. Black ironwork. White lettering shaded sblack

Figure 4

Source: Sketch by P. Matthews

LLANDINAM

Richard Griffiths

Wagon No.1 hired from Birmingham RC&W Co. from December 1886 to December 1890.

LLANFAIR CAEREINION

J Ll Peate & Sons *(Figure 5 overleaf)*

This firm was unusual, perhaps unique in Wales, in owning both standard and narrow gauge wagons. The standard gauge wagons could, of course, approach no nearer to Llanfair than Welshpool but the office and depot were situated in Llanfair.

As well as coal the firm dealt in lime, obtaining up to 300 tons of lime per season from the Porthywaen Lime Co. works at Llanymynech. Apparently Llanymynech lime was preferred in the Llanfair area to that produced at Llynclys, Nantmawr or Porthywaen. The business is known to have been in existence by 1889/90.

The standard gauge wagons were numbered 1, 3 and 4 while the narrow gauge ones were numbered 2, 5, 6, 7 and 8 and were of 4T capacity and built by R Y Pickering & Co.

Livery was maroon with white lettering and possibly the ironwork was black.

There is a photograph in *The Welshpool & Llanfair Light Railway*.[6]

Unfortunately I have been unable to discover any details of the standard gauge wagons but the lettering was probably the same as that of the narrow gauge ones.

LLANFYLLIN

Llanfyllin Coal & Lime Co. *(Figure 6 overleaf)*

This company was formed by Thomas Jones, David Rowlands, R F Evans and David Edwards, who was the manager during 1889/90.

Wagon No.1, a 6-tonner, was hired on 18th August 1873 from Birmingham RC&W Co. and returned in September 1877, the hiring charge being £11pa.

Wagons Nos.3 and 4, also 6 Tons, were purchased over seven years from 21st March 1881 at £5 5s 0d pa and were second-hand.

Besides coal wagons, the company also operated lime wagons and was still extant in 1926.

Plate 7 - B.Q.C., Llanelwedd

B.Q.C. No.987 initially belonged to J Arnold & Sons, Chipping Sodbury. It was registered by the GWR in 1924 as 47675 but came into the orbit of B.Q.C. when that company was set up about 1930.

Note 'NONPOOL' annotation.

Courtesy Don Rees

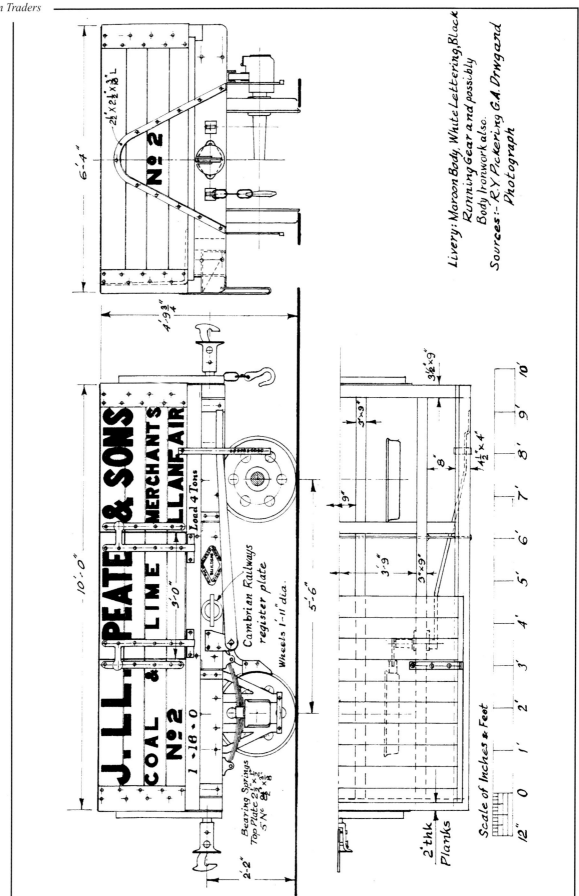

Figure 5

Livery: Maroon Body, White Lettering, Black
Running Gear and possibly
Body Ironwork also.
Sources:- R.Y. Pickering G.A. Drwgard
Photograph

No 2

6'-4"

J.L.PEATE & SONS
MERCHANTS
LLANFAIR
LIME
COAL &
No 2
Load 4 Tons

Cambrian Railways
register plate

Wheels 1'-11" dia.

10'-0"
3'-0"
1-18-0
2'-2"
4'-9¾"
5'-6"

2½"x2½"x⅜" L

Bearing Springs
Top Plate 2½"x½"
5 N° 2½"x⅜"

2"thk
Planks

3½"x9"
3"x9"
8"
9"
3'-9"
3'-9"
3"x9"
4½"x4"

Scale of Inches & Feet
12" 0   1' 2' 3' 4' 5' 6' 7' 8' 9' 10'

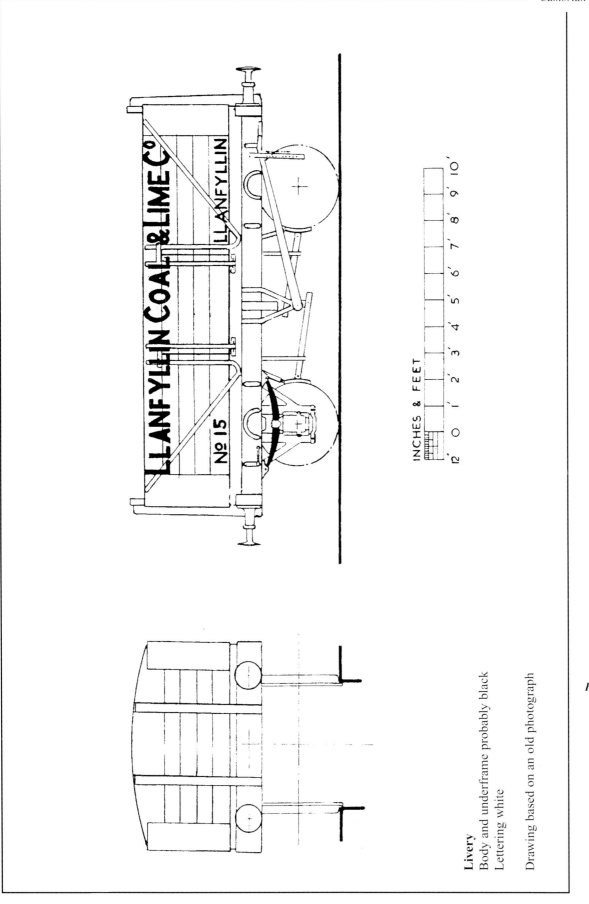

INCHES & FEET

Livery
Body and underframe probably black
Lettering white

Drawing based on an old photograph

Figure 6

LLANIDLOES

John Godfrey Wienholt Bowen

Wagon No.1, 6 Tons, hired between July 1888 and September 1892 from Birmingham RC&W Co.

Morgan & Son

Wagons hired from Birmingham RC&W Co. were:

Nos.1 and 2 between May 1883 and October 1888; Nos.3 and 4 between July 1885 and October 1888.

A D Morgan & Son was still trading in 1934.

LLANRHAIADR

J E Vaughan

Presumably this firm obtained its wagons after the opening of the TVLR in 1904.

In a photograph of a Staffordshire colliery a high sided open wagon, partly obscured, can be made out lettered 'J.E.Vaughan'.

LLANYMYNECH

D Evans

Address given as Newbridge Wharf, near Llanymynech. Wagon No.1, 8 Tons, hired from 1st December 1864 to October 1869 from Birmingham RC&W Co.

Also at Llanymynech was Savin & Co. but for the sake of brevity this company will be dealt with under Porthywaen.

Plate 8 - Savin & Co. (possibly)

The remains of an old dumb-buffer wagon in the yard at Porthywaen. The photograph was taken in 1952 but the foreman at the yard said the wagon body had been in the same position for 50 years. It started life as an open wagon, the makeshift roof being added when it was converted to store salt.

M Lloyd collection

LLYNCLYS

Llynclys Lime Works

The company was still listed in 1917. One of their wagons may be seen on page 77 of _Cambrian Railways Album_.[3A]

Montgomeryshire Coal & Lime Co.

This company was part of the Savin empire and may not have been operated from Llynclys although the office was there. It had a depot at Llanidloes in 1880 with Hugh Mills as Agent.

The company hired nineteen 8T wagons numbered 71-89 from the Birmingham RC&W Co. from August/October 1865 until October/December 1872.

In April 1868 twenty 10T wagons Nos.120-139 were acquired through a hire purchase agreement completed in 1875. Another 10T wagon, No.144, was bought under a similar agreement between August 1869 and 1873.

Savin & Co. _(Plate 8)_

Porthywaen Lime Co. _(Figures 7-11)_

Steetley Co. Ltd. _(Figures 12, 13; plates 9, 10, 11)_

Thomas Savin was a prime example of a Victorian entrepreneur pushing his enterprises to their limit and sometimes beyond, as with his railway interests. He appears to have become interested in the quarries at Llynclys and Llanymynech in the early 1860s. The scope of his other enterprises may be judged from a letter-heading of 1868 which read

'Porthywaen, Llanymynech, Coedygoe, Fenn's Bank and Ynyslas; Lime, Limestone, Coal, Brick, and Tile Works'.

Savin died in 1889. About 1897 Savin & Co. formed a partnership with a Captain Nicholson; this partnership traded as the Porthywaen Lime Co. Ltd. The change of name was not without its perils. When its representative called at a firm in Saltney to find out why it had failed to win a contract he was told that had the firm known that they were the late Savin & Co. they might have been successful, but they did know who Porthywaen Lime Co. were and wanted a sample truck of lime.

Until the early 1900s the rock quarried was calcium limestone which was burnt in the kiln to produce burnt lime or hydrated lime. While some of this material was used for agricultural purposes, most of it was used for iron and steel making in the Midlands and South Wales. In the early 1900s dolomite limestone, on account of its magnesium content, was discovered to be a valuable ingredient in the manufacture of steel and gradually it took preference over the quarrying of calcium limestone.

The result of this discovery was the formation of a new company called The Porthywaen Lime and Basic Co. Ltd. This company lasted until 1932 when it was taken over by the Steetley Lime and Building Stone Co. of Worksop and re-named Steetley Lime and Basic Co. In 1944 there was another change, this time to Steetley Co. Ltd. The limestone quarries at Llanymynech ceased operating at the outbreak of World War I.

It would appear that in the 1870s Savin & Co. depended largely on the Cambrian to supply suitable wagons for the transport of limestone and in 1870 the railway company owned 366 wagons classified as lime wagons. However, it appears from correspondence which has survived that the Cambrian was unable to supply wagons when most required and the burnt limestone was stacked outside the kilns and men laid off.

After hiring wagons for short periods from the Potteries, Shrewsbury and North Wales Railway, Savin & Co. began to steadily build up a fleet of their own wagons. Details of Savin & Co.'s wagons

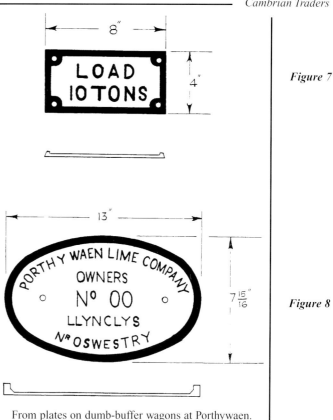

Figure 7

Figure 8

From plates on dumb-buffer wagons at Porthywaen.

Plate 9 - Steetley Co. Ltd.

This old wagon was located in the yard at Porthywaen and is interesting for a couple of reasons. The sides have been lowered as can be seen by the marks left by the original diagonal strapping seen on the right hand end. This was probably done at the same time as the wagon was converted to sprung buffers.

On the other side of the wagon a cast plate carried 'Converted 1905 by Harrison & Camm Rotherham'. Faded white lettering stated 'Empty to / Steetley Siding / M.S.& L. or Mid Ry'.

M Lloyd collection

are scarce; the only drawing I have been able to locate is one of a lime wagon in the Birmingham Public Library.[47] The wagon was built by Brown Marshall & Co. probably in the 1860/70s.

Typical of the period it had dumb buffers and was 14ft 0in long by 7ft 6in wide externally. It had a ridged, or cottage top as it was called in the trade, giving a height of 5ft 8in from the floor in the centre. The wheel-base was 8ft 0in.

Unfortunately no details of livery or lettering is known. Probably the lettering followed the style of the period, the name of the company occupying almost the depth of one plank.

A probable Savin wagon survived in the yard at Porthywaen until the mid-1960s. This was a 3-plank dumb-buffered wagon 15ft 6in long by 7ft 6in wide externally which still carried a Porthywaen Lime Co. plate and was numbered 15. Perhaps because of a sudden surge in demand, or for some other reason, Savin & Co. hired forty wagons from the Birmingham RC&W Co. from February/August 1888 to December 1888/February 1889. They were numbered 220-259.

When the Porthywaen Lime Co. was formed in 1897 wagons were re-lettered, not always with the desired result. *(See Figure 9 opposite)* The lettering shows the range of products the company dealt in. To deal with this variety of traffic the Porthywaen Lime Co. had various types of wagons ranging from low sided open to coal wagons, coke wagons and, of course, lime wagons.

In 1897 the company obtained a quote from J H Ketley & Co. Ltd. of Globe Wagon Works, Stoke-on-Trent, for converting some of their open wagons into covered wagons. A year later the matter appears to have been still under discussion and a price of £6 per wagon was mentioned. While this conversion was being considered, a quote was obtained from the Midland RC&W Co. Ltd. for 20-30 covered wagons at £54 10s 0d each or £9 11s 9d per annum for seven years deferred payment. Unfortunately the remaining records fail to show whether these quotes were taken up.

The early wagons had wooden underframes but later ones were built with steel framing. The company had its own wagon repair shop at Porthywaen. It had its own smithy and, when I visited the site in the late 1950s, large pigeon holes held stencils for the Steetley lettering.

Plate 10 - Steetley Co. Ltd.

Built for the Porthywaen Lime Co. by the Midland RC&W Co. in 1898 and registered by the Cambrian.

M Lloyd collection

Plate 11 - Steetley Co. Ltd.

Wagons Nos.560 and 535 were very similar to No.527 but were built with a steel channel underframe with solebars 9in deep. Built by Midland RC&W Co. about 1912.

M Lloyd collection

PORTHYWAEN LIME Co. LTD

A

PORTHYWAEN LIME Cº LIMITED		
LIME		LIMESTONE
MACADAM		CHIPPINGS
Nº		
TARE		Empty to Llynclys Cambrian Rly

Proposed lettering for Railway trucks

A. Proposed lettering for Porthywaen Lime Co. wagons 1897

B

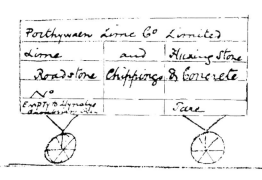

B. Lettering on first six wagons

Figure 9

Source

Copies of sketches enclosed with letter from H Le Neve Foster, Birmingham, to E O Nicholson, Llynclys, 6th April 1897

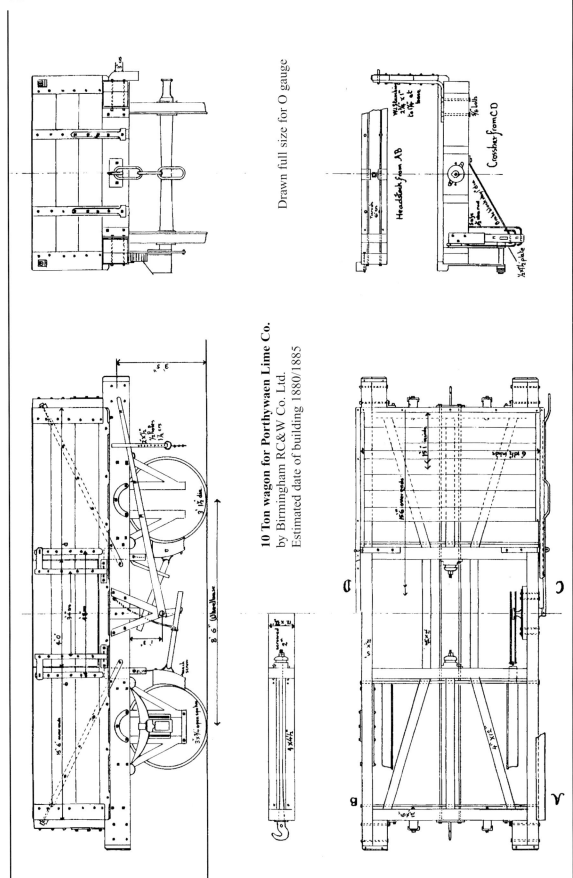

Drawn full size for O gauge

10 Ton wagon for Porthywaen Lime Co.
by Birmingham RC&W Co. Ltd.
Estimated date of building 1880/1885

Figure 10

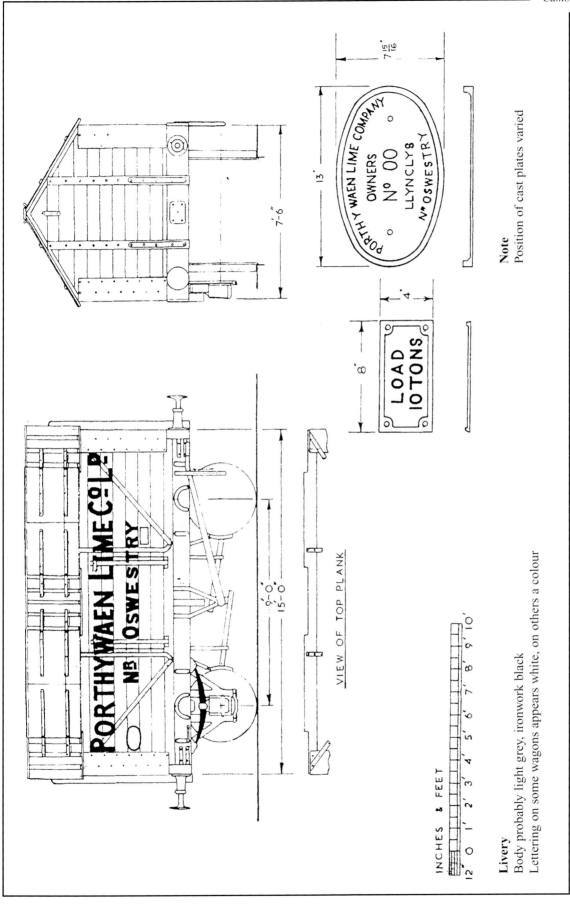

7'15/16

13'

PORTHY WAEN LIME COMPANY
OWNERS
Nº 00
LLYNCLYS
Nª OSWESTRY

4"

8'

LOAD
10 TONS

Note
Position of cast plates varied

7'-6"

PORTHYWAEN LIME Cº Lᴰ
Nᴮ OSWESTRY

9'-0"
15'-0"

VIEW OF TOP PLANK

INCHES & FEET
12 0 1' 2' 3' 4' 5' 6' 7' 8' 9' 10'

Livery
Body probably light grey, ironwork black
Lettering on some wagons appears white, on others a colour

Figure 11

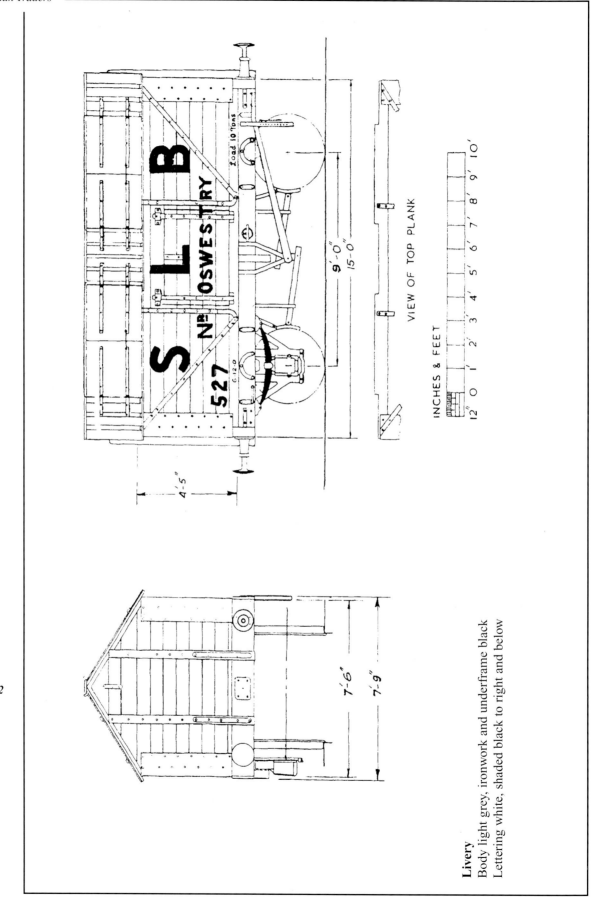

Figure 12

VIEW OF TOP PLANK

INCHES & FEET

Livery
Body light grey, ironwork and underframe black
Lettering white, shaded black to right and below

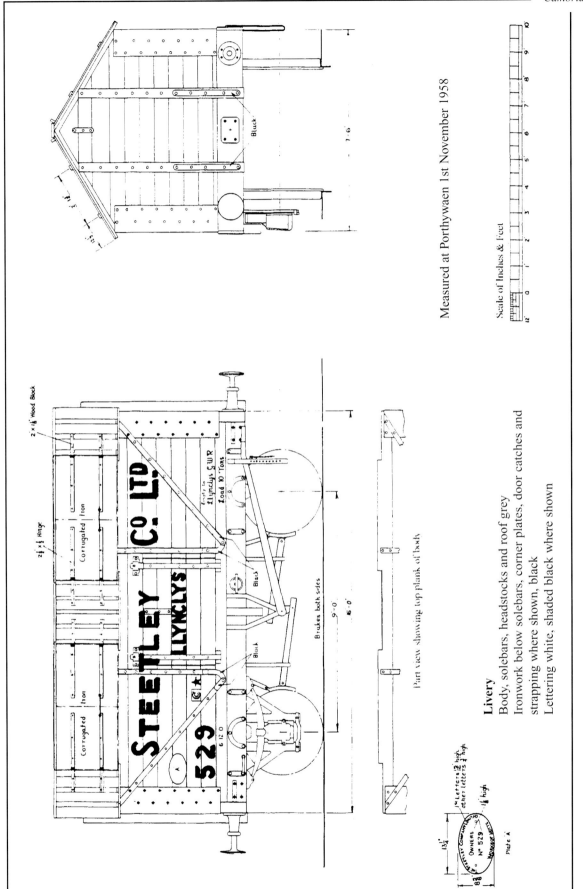

Measured at Porthywaen 1st November 1958

Scale of Inches & Feet

Part view showing top plank of body

Livery

Body, solebars, headstocks and roof grey
Ironwork below solebars, corner plates, door catches and
strapping where shown, black
Lettering white, shaded black where shown

Figure 13

MACHYNLLETH

Edward Davies *(Plate 12)*

This owner appears to have operated in the 1880/90s, as other owners whose memories went back to before World War I were unable to recall him. An Edward Davies of Dolcaradog had mining interests in the area in the late 1850s.

Was this the same Edward Davies whose name appears on Photograph 514 in the Gloucester RC&W Co. collection? It shows 5-plank, open wagon No.5 with internal dimensions of 14ft 0in x 6ft 11in x 3ft 41/2in, sprung buffers and single-sided brake gear.

Richard Evans

One wagon No.2 hired March 1884 to March 1885 from the Birmingham RC&W Co.

J Lumley *(Plate 13)*

A long-established firm, known to be in existence in 1881, which owned six wagons. An unusual feature of wagon No.21 was the darker colouring of the third plank down. This odd-coloured plank seems to have been a fashion of the period. Lumley & Son wagon No.22 is seen in photograph B7497 of Dinas Mawddwy in the Welsh Industrial & Maritime Museum's collection.

Robert Pugh *(Figure 14 & Plate 14)*

This was another long established Machynlleth firm. It was started by Robert Pugh, probably in the 1880s, then carried on by his son Hugh who, in his turn, passed it on to his son R E Pugh. The latter died in 1935 after which the business was carried on by his widow until 1956.

This firm had two wagons at one time but one was smashed during shunting. No.8 was built by W Rigley of Bulwell. Their coal supplies were mostly obtained from collieries at Ford Green, Sneyd and Chatterley (NSR) but also some from the Wrexham coalfield.

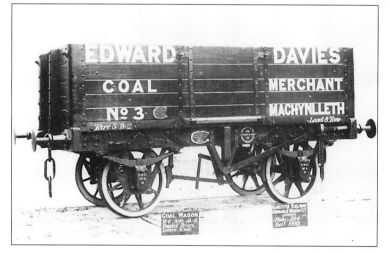

Plate 12 - *Edward Davies, Machynlleth*

This wagon was registered in 1888 as an 8 Ton wagon by the GWR, No.74. Edward Davies hired this wagon from the Gloucester RC&W Co.

Courtesy HMRS

Plate 13 - *Hugh Lumley, Machynlleth*

A photograph showing three proud generations of the Lumley family standing by one of their wagons. The livery was probably grey with the third plank from top likely to be red with white lettering, shaded black. Ironwork was black. Note end of Cambrian Railways goods brake on right with the inverted 'V' stanchion.

Courtesy Huw Lumley

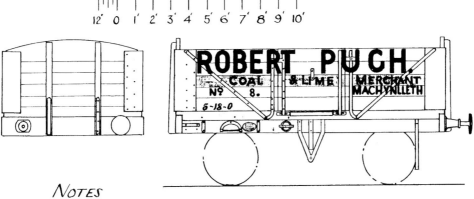

Figure 14

NOTES
1. Built 1901 by W. Rigley, Bulwell, Nottingham. Commandeered during 1939-45 war.
2. Painted grey, shaded plank probably red or dark grey. Iron work black. Lettering white shaded black. Tare not shaded. Wheel rims white when built.
3. Brake lever and two brake shoes on one side only.
4. Drawing based on photograph and estimated dimensions.
5. Split spoked wheels.
6. Registered by Cambrian Railways

RT
TYPICAL SHADING

Plate 14 - Robert Pugh, Machynlleth

An official photograph of wagon No.8 built in 1901 by W Rigley, Bulwell, Nottingham and lent to me by Mrs Mary Pugh. She was the widow of the late Robert Pugh, coal merchant, and carried on the business until 1956 after her husband's death. Later she was thrilled to see a model that I had built of their wagon.

Livery was probably grey with a red plank, white lettering shaded black and black ironwork.

Courtesy Mrs Mary Pugh

MINFFORDD

Pwllheli Granite Co. *(Figure 15 & Plate 15)*

This company had its origins in the 1850s when Carreg-y-Imbill, or Gimlet Rock to give it its English name, was worked by the Liverpool and Pwllheli Granite Co. This company mostly produced granite setts for roads but large blocks of stone were also quarried for building purposes.

When the company started operating there was no railway at Pwllheli and the output was taken away by ships. Although Gimlet Rock was still being worked in the 1880/1890s (by Brundrett & Co. of Penmaenmawr), I have been unable to discover any evidence of stone being loaded at Pwllheli. By this time the quarry at Minffordd was being worked and that had a connection to the Cambrian Railways.

In August 1912 the company purchased forty 10T wagons from the Birmingham RC&W Co. numbered 121-145 with tare weights ranging from 5-17-3 to 6-1-3. The wagons were 14ft 6in x 7ft x 2ft 2in internally and had brakes on both sides.

While photographs of the early 1920s would suggest a grey livery, J P Richards has recorded that the wagons were painted red oxide. Lettering was white and the corner plates, at least, may have been black. When wagons were repainted with the lettering diagonal, J P R gives the livery as black.

Peter Matthews, in *Private Owner Wagons* [25], has a drawing of a 5-plank open wagon No.167. The top part of a similar wagon may be seen in a photograph of Oswestry in the Shropshire Records & Research Unit, Ref. 3966/Misc/2/32. In a sketch of a 5-plank open, which Peter Matthews sent to the writer, he describes the livery as dark grey, white lettering and black ironwork.

Syenite Paving Sets Quarry Co. Ltd.

This was a short lived concern in the 1870s. The quarry was situated on Moel Ystradau about 1¼ miles south of Blaenau Ffestiniog and was served by a siding which left the narrow gauge Festiniog Railway just north of Moelwyn Tunnel. From January to April 1878 the company hired 11 wagons from the Birmingham RC&W Co. numbered 1 to 11. It is just possible that these were narrow gauge wagons but more likely they were standard gauge, the setts being transported to Minfordd by the FR and there transferred into standard wagons.

NANTMAWR

Chirk Castle Lime Co.

The main plant and quarry were situated at Whitehurst (formerly Llangollen Road) on the down side of the GWR Gobowen to Chester line. At some date, probably in the 1930s, the company took over the working of the quarry at Nantmawr from the Lilleshall Co. and some stone was taken from there to Froncysyllte to be made into tarmacadam.

Lilleshall Co. *(Plate 16)*

This company was established at Donnington, to the north east of Wellington, in 1764, where it operated collieries and iron-works. At first it obtained its limestone locally but flooding in the quarries encouraged the company to go further afield for supplies. In the late 1860s they took a lease of land at Much Wenlock for quarrying and later took over the Nantmawr quarry from Richard Samuel France, one of the promoters of the Potteries, Shrewsbury & North Wales Railway.

In 1913 the Lilleshall Co. obtained 10T wagons from the Gloucester RC&W Co., lettered 'Empty to Nantmawr'. A history of the company states that 50 new main line wagons were bought in 1918 bringing the main line stock to 200 wagons while another 250 were employed on internal traffic. The figure of 200 would have included the wagons allocated to Donnington where most, if not all, the internal wagons would have been. In 1901 the Lilleshall Co. had a contract for the supply of coal to the Cambrian as well as to the GWR and LNWR.

Plate 15 - Pwllheli Granite Co.

A view at Barmouth showing the livery used from the early 1920s. Opinions vary as to the body colours of Pwllheli Granite Co. wagons but Jim Richards, who took this photograph, says that in this case it was black.

Courtesy J P Richards

NEWTOWN

John Evans

Wagon No.4 is illustrated in *Private Owner Wagons* by Bill Hudson.[34] The caption states that there is a diagonal plate on the solebar indicating that it had been converted from dumb-buffers. I have been unable to trace John Evans in the trade directories that I have consulted.

Thomas Parry Jones

Wagons numbered 3, 4, 5 & 6 purchased 1881 from Birmingham RC&W Co.

Herbert Lewis Matthews

Wagons numbered 1 & 2 purchased August 1883 from Birmingham RC&W Co.

W Morris & Sons

Wagon No.1 built appropriately by the Cambrian Wagon Co. Ltd. in 1922. Livery was red oxide with black ironwork and white lettering.

Drg: MRN Jul 1969 p352.

W R Parry

Wagons numbered 1 to 3 hired between November 1882 and April 1883 from Birmingham RC&W Co.

Emily Catherine Schofield

Two 8T wagons Nos.1 and 2 hired from June 1885 until November 1889 from Birmingham RC&W Co.

OSWESTRY

As the GWR arrived in Oswestry some 15 years before the Cambrian a well developed coal trade had been established at the GWR station and most coal merchants in the town were located there. Some merchants, J Huxley and Sons being an example, although located at the GWR wharf also had depots at the Cambrian stations.

N Davies

Wagon No.1, 7T, hired from January 1864 to January 1869 from Birmingham RC&W Co. The company is not listed in the 1870 trade directory.

William Edwards

Nineteen 10T wagons numbered E8 to E26 and 47 8T wagons numbered 28 to 74 (no E prefix) hired between November 1888 and January 1894 from Birmingham RC&W Co. The number of wagons involved suggest that Edwards was something more than a coal merchant, perhaps a contractor!

Griffiths & Jones

Wagons numbers 11 and 12 hired between 1876 and 1879 from Birmingham RC&W Co.

Hughes, Lloyd & Clare

Wagons numbered 1 & 2 hired 1868 - 1871 from Birmingham RC&W Co. In the directory for 1870 a Robert Clare is listed as a coal merchant, furniture van owner and beer retailer at the GW Wharf and Pool Rd.

J Huxley & Co.

An 1885 directory lists Huxley Bros. but the 1891 edition names J Huxley & Co. By 1922 the title had changed to J Huxley and Sons and appears under that name in the 1926 RCH Handbook. Although his main depot was on the GW Wharf, Oswestry, he also had depots at Llynclys, Llanyblodwell, (Blodwell Junction) and Four Crosses on the Cambrian as well as Kinnerley and Nesscliffe on the S&MR. He advertised North & South Staffordshire and Welsh coals of all descriptions. He also dealt in lime, manure and salt.

William Jenkinson

A contractor who hired two 8T wagons numbered 100 and 101 from the Birmingham RC&W Co. for the period April 1911 to December 1912.

Plate 16 - Lilleshall Co., Nantmawr

Built by the Gloucester RC&W Co. and registered by the GWR in February 1914. The wagon and its sisters were used for carrying limestone from quarries and kilns at Nantmawr to Donnington.

The colour described as red may mean red oxide, lettering white. The ironwork with the exception of the diagonals appears to be black.

Courtesy HMRS

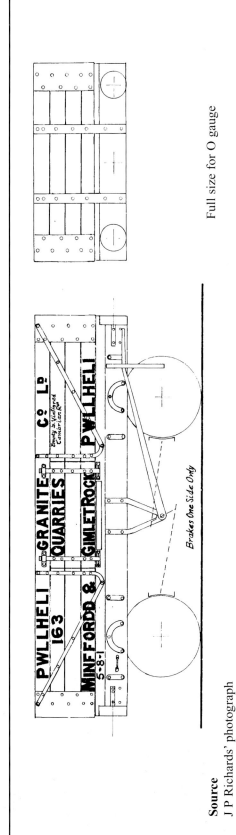

Figure 15

Full size for O gauge

Brakes One Side Only

Source
J P Richards' photograph
Dimensions estimated

W Martin & Co.

A long-established firm who purchased two wagons, numbers 2 and 4 in February 1875 and November 1879 respectively, from the Birmingham RC&W Co. The firm, whose depot was on the Cambrian wharf, closed in the mid-1960s.

T Milner *(Figure 16)*

Apparently a late-comer as I have been unable to find him in any directory up to 1922. However, he appears in the RCH Commuted Annual Payout Arrangement for January 1926.

He operated from the GWR wharf and his wagons were lettered 'Tom Milner'.

James Nurse *(Figure 17)*

Listed in directories for 1891 and 1900 but probably had a longer existence. There is a photograph in *Oswestry Railways.*[24]

George Rogers

Listed in the 1885 directory as having his depot on the GWR wharf. He hired two wagons from the Birmingham RC&W Co. from September 1882 to October 1884.

E Shepherd *(Plate 17)*

As mentioned in the Introduction Shepherd appears in the directory for 1900 only. Wagon No.1 was built by Renshaw and Co. As will be seen from the photograph it has provision for the contents to be covered with a tarpaulin.

W H Thomas & Sons Ltd.

Listed in the RCH handbooks for 1926 and 1933.

Williams & Wilson *(Figure 18)*

Listed in directories of 1900 and 1922 and in RCH Handbook for 1933. Traded from the GWR wharf.

Jos. Williams & Son Ltd. *(Plate 18 overleaf)*

A firm of long standing, appearing as early as 1885 and closing in the late 1960s. The firm used the Cambrian wharf. An enquiry to the firm in 1968 elicited the information that wagons belonging to William Blake, Hereford, were to be seen in Oswestry.

Williams hired 22 wagons from the Birmingham RC&W Co. between April 1883 and October 1891. Wagon No.134 was purchased from the Gloucester RC&W Co. in 1914 and according to script on the wagon side, coal was obtained from Littleton Colliery.

Other evidence shows that coal was also obtained from the Sneyd and Madeley Wood Collieries.

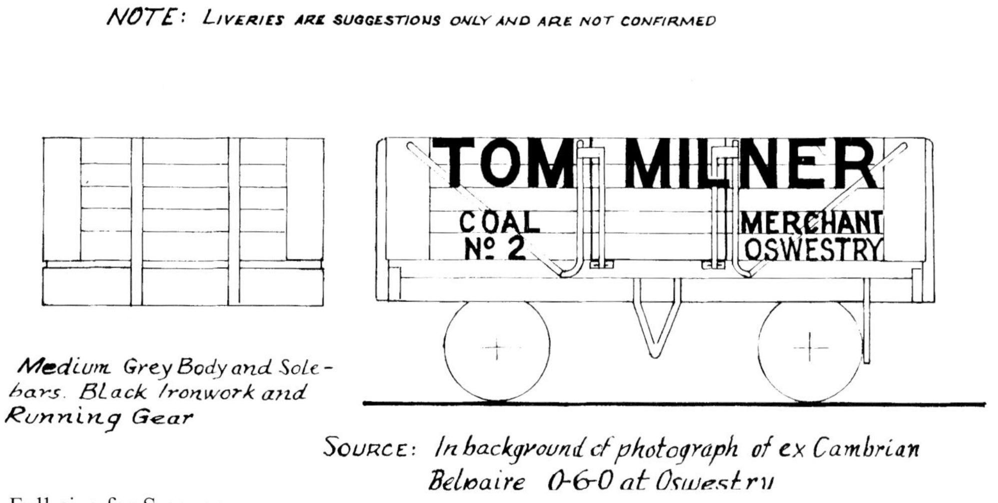

NOTE: LIVERIES ARE SUGGESTIONS ONLY AND ARE NOT CONFIRMED

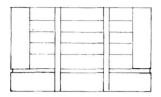

TOM MILNER
COAL
No 2
MERCHANT
OSWESTRY

Medium Grey Body and Solebars. Black Ironwork and
Running Gear

SOURCE: In background of photograph of ex Cambrian
Belpaire 0-6-0 at Oswestry

Figure 16

Full size for S gauge

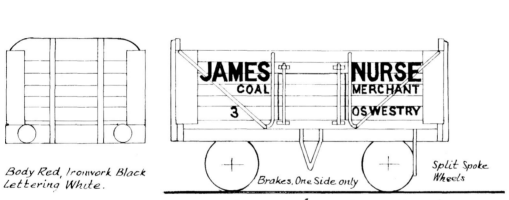

JAMES NURSE
COAL
3
MERCHANT
OSWESTRY

*Body Red, Ironwork Black
Lettering White.*

Brakes, One Side only

Split Spoke
Wheels

SOURCE: Photograph in "Oswestry Railways".
Pub. Bridge Books, Wrexham.

Figure 17

Full size for S gauge

ERNEST SHEPHERD
BUILDERS MERCHANT. SLATES, BRICKS, CEMENT, CONCRETE PAVING FLAGS.
MACHADAM & CHIPPINGS. OSWESTRY No 1
5-8-2 Empty to

Plate 17 - Ernest Shepherd, Oswestry

*An interesting wagon built for a short lived firm by W R
Renshaw & Co. of Stoke on Trent. Note the horizontal rail
between the ends so that a sheet could be used to protect
materials such as cement against the elements.*

Courtesy B H Holland

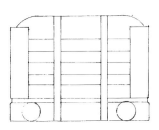

Figure 18

Medium Grey Body and Solebars Black Corner Plates, Vertical Strapping (But not Diagonal) Fittings on Solebars and Running Gear. Lettering White, shaded Black on Names

SOURCE: Photograph, Ref. 3966/Misc/2/32. Shropshire Records & Research Unit.

Full size for S gauge

As the firm was a colliery agent their wagons would have been seen over much of the Cambrian and a photograph taken in the 1930s shows one of their wagons at Llanfyllin.

PENRHYNDEUDRAETH

John Roberts

Wagon or wagons hired from Birmingham RC&W Co. between November 1887 and January 1891.

John Edward Williams *(Plate 19)*

Wagon No.1, an eight-tonner, was hired from the Birmingham RC&W Co. from 1910 until after 1914. He is listed in the RCH book for 1933 and the telephone directory for 1968. By good fortune Jim Richards photographed wagon No.1 at Barmouth in the early 1920s.

PENYBONTFAWR

F Ambrose

Although the earliest reference I have found to this merchant as having wagons is in the 1926 RCH Handbook, other records show that he was in business in 1900 as a general merchant using Llynclys Station as his railhead. Perhaps he added coal to his business when the TVLR appeared in 1904.

PORTHYWAEN

For Porthywaen Lime Co., SLB and Steetley Lime Co. see Llynclys.

John Robert Williams

The above gentleman, acting as administrator to the estate of the late Mary Elizabeth Williams, Porthywaen Lime Works, Oswestry, hired 33 10T wagons, Nos.1 to 33 from Birmingham RC&W Co. from November 1871 to August 1872; all of them were purchased by March/August 1872.

Mary Williams is listed at the lime works in the 1870 directory, the same directory that also lists Thomas Savin's lime works. The question arises as to whether the Porthywaen Lime Works mentioned above is the same works of which Savin became the owner.

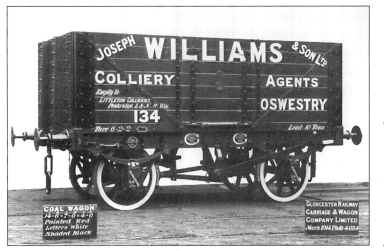

Plate 18 - Joseph Williams & Son Ltd., Oswestry

This was built by the Gloucester RC&W Co. in 1914 and registered by the Cambrian.

Littleton Colliery was situated between Penkridge and Gailey on the line between Stafford and Wolverhampton.

Courtesy HMRS

PORTMADOC

Robert Hughes

Two wagons, Nos.4 and 6, built by Birmingham RC&W Co. and sold on to R Richards & Son sometime between 1903 and 1910.

John Jones

Two wagons, Nos.1 and 2, hired from Birmingham RC&W Co. from 1875 to 1876.

The Pensyflog Iron Mining Co.

A short-lived venture which was incorporated on 8th July 1872 and wound up on 30th January 1874. The mine was situated 600 yards north-west of the Cambrian station (OS reference SH562395) and was served by a siding off the Gorseddau Tramway.

Ten wagons were hired from Birmingham RC&W Co. for the period October 1872 to January 1874. As the mine had a narrow gauge rail connection there is a possibility that these were narrow gauge wagons.

Ref: 'Narrow Gauge Railways in South Caernarvonshire' p34. [7]

Ellis Williams

The company is listed in Slater's Directory of 1880. Eight wagons, Nos.14 to 21, were hired from Birmingham RC&W Co. but no dates available.

PWLLHELI

Eifionyd Farmers Association Ltd.

Peter Matthews, in *Private Owner Wagons* [25], illustrates wagon No.17 belonging to this company. It is of 10 tons capacity and the side is made up of seven planks.

Livery is given as medium grey, all ironwork black but ends of brake levers were white. Lettering was white shaded black.

An enquiry to the firm in 1992 elicited the response that they did not know that they had owned wagons! (Stephen Bell)

Evan Williams

2, Salem Terrace, hired four wagons, Nos.1, 2, 3 and 5, from Birmingham RC&W Co. from August 1879 until March 1888.

RHAYADER

Rhayader Granite Quarries Ltd.

From an order placed in May 1912, twelve wagons were hired from July/August 1912 from Birmingham RC&W Co. The wagons, Nos.5, 10, 15, 20, 25, 30, 35, 40, 45, 50, 55 and 60 were returned because the firm went bankrupt and subsequently sold to Field & Mackay Ltd. of Ludlow on 7th December 1912. One record states they were of 10T capacity with oak underframes but the order book states 12T granite wagons.

TOWYN

Lewis Edwards

Wagon No.1 purchased from Birmingham RC&W Co. in 1888.

John Humphries

Wagon No.3 purchased in 1879 from Birmingham RC&W Co.

Morris Jones and Sons

The company is listed in 1926 RCH Handbook. Their 4-plank open No.4 is shown an the Aberdovey Harbour Branch in 1914 in C C Green's *The Coast Lines of the Cambrian Vol.2.* [3]

Tonfanau Granite Quarries *(Plate 20 overleaf)*

This quarry was situated at Tonfanau just over 2 miles to the north of Towyn. It was started about 1895 by John Corbett MP, who resided at Ynysmaengwyn, near Towyn. A 2ft. gauge tramway about a half mile long was laid between the quarry and a transhipment siding on the coast line.

Plate 19 - John E Williams, Penrhyndeudraeth

A nice one for the lettering enthusiast! The photograph was taken at Barmouth by Jim Richards as the wagon was on its way north. Unfortunately, Jim is unsure about the body colour - black or red. On the original print there is a hint of shading so I am inclined to believe it was the latter.

R.S.O. stands for 'Railway Sub Office' and was part of a postal address.

Courtesy J P Richards

Industrial Locomotives of North Wales [21] published by the Industrial Railway Society records that a vertical boilered locomotive *Freda* worked the tramway. About 1906 the quarry was acquired by a Mr Gibbons who replaced the tramway by a standard gauge siding which the Cambrian agreed to work.[3]

From 1920 the title changed to Tonfanau Granite Quarries Ltd. and later became a subsidiary of Penmaenmawr Welsh Granite Co. Ltd.

Three- and four-planked dropside wagons lettered 'Tonfanau Granite Quarries, Towyn, Merioneth' were used by the quarry. Peter Matthews recorded an 8T 3-plank open with a centre drop door. The livery is given as black with white lettering.

Plate 20 - Tonfanau Granite Quarries

A view taken in 1922 showing quarry company wagons being shunted under the stone crushers at Tonfanau. Another version of the lettering appears in 'Cambrian Railways Album' Vol.1 p71.

Courtesy H B Evans and C C Green

WELSHPOOL

A E Breeze

As this firm's depot was situated at Holly Bush Wharf on the Montgomeryshire Canal it seems likely that the business pre-dated the coming of the railway. Presumably after the railway arrived most, if not all, of his coal was brought in by train. However, in the RCH Handbook for 1926 the address is still given as Holly Bush Wharf.

A goods receipt, reproduced in *The Archaeology of the Montgomeryshire Canal* [8], advertises that the company dealt in Cannock Chase, Wigan, Ruabon, Harwood and Wrexham Coals as well as building materials and flower pots. Additionally he was an agent for fire, life and insurance companies. The 1933 RCH Handbook gives the name as Breeze Bros. at the same address.

The Farmers, Lime, Coal & General Supply Co. Welch Pool *(sic)*

Twenty wagons hired from Birmingham RC&W Co. from October 1870 to October 1872, numbered 31 to 50.

W E Morgan *(Plate 21)*

He is listed in the 1926 and 1933 RCH Handbooks but was almost certainly in business earlier than that. Wagon No.1 built Midland RC&W Co. It was a 10T 5-plank open with slightly raised ends.

J & M Morris Ltd.

This firm was established in 1835 and, besides being colliery agents, dealt in agricultural machinery, ironmongery and seeds and is listed in RCH Handbooks for 1926 and 1933. When contacted in 1968 they regretted that they had no records of their wagons.

John Norris

Address given as Mill Lane foundry so was probably an iron founder. Two 8T wagons, Nos.1 and 2, were hired from Birmingham RC&W Co. from February 1873.

Owen & Hamer

The Directory for 1880 lists George Hamer, 15 Severn St. Two wagons, Nos.1 and 3, hired from Birmingham RC&W Co. from 1878 until 1881.

Parry, Son & Parry

The company was also at Newtown. Four 8T wagons, Nos.1 to 4, hired between November 1872 and October 1876 from Birmingham RC&W Co.

Ll Peate & Sons - *See Llanfair Caereinion.*

Plate 21 - W E Morgan, Welshpool

An official photograph of a 10T wagon built by the Midland RC&W Co for W E Morgan. The livery was probably grey with white lettering, shaded black, and with black ironwork.

M Lloyd collection

Chapter 4

Discovering Foreign Visitors to the Cambrian

Scarcity of Information

As with the home-based wagons it is impossible to be definitive about private owner wagons from outside the Cambrian system. The position would have changed periodically as contracts expired and new ones came into operation. However, a general picture can be presented which will give an indication of which foreign wagons might have been seen on the Cambrian.

This account is heavily biased towards the history of wagons received at Llynclys and Porthywaen, and to a lesser extent Doldowlod, simply because the information has been available. The Llynclys wagon invoice book for 1899/1900, memos for the same period and wagon labels have provided an immense amount of information not only for Llynclys, but Porthywaen and Western Wharf as well.

The last two places came under control of the Llynclys Station Master or Agent as he was titled on the Cambrian.

Nearly all of the loads for Western Wharf were for the Sweeney Blue Brick Co. The information for Doldowlod comes from a list compiled by the late John Stratton for the years 1916/1917. The remainder of the information has nearly all come from photographs and, in one or two cases, recollections of old railwaymen or merchants.

Early Visitors to the Cambrian

The earliest mention I have found of a foreign PO wagon on the Cambrian is in *Coal Trade Wagons* [1] where mention is made of a salt wagon that broke an axle at Cemmes Road in 1868.

Although many of the coal merchants possessed their own wagons, often they were insufficient to cope with their trade and wagons belonging to a colliery or coal factor would have brought in their supplies. Other coal merchants depended entirely on their supplies reaching them in such wagons. This position would seem to apply in particular to the Mid-Wales line as the only coal wagon owners I have been able to find are at Llanidloes.

Coal merchants, both those with and without their own wagons, received supplies from several different collieries, probably reflecting the different types of coal.

For instance, S Williams of Llynclys who, as far as I know, did not have his own wagons, received in a space of eighteen months coal from: Ruabon Coal &

Coke Co. Ltd., Vauxhall Colliery, Westminster Colliery, Donnington Colliery (owned by the Lilleshall Co.) and Stafford Coal & Iron Co. Ltd.

On occasions coal and stone arrived in railway company wagons, the former mostly in Midland Railway vehicles. To give a couple of examples, nine MR wagons conveyed 72t 15cwt. of coal from Swansea to Porthywaen via Brecon in February 1900. A more intriguing example were the two loads in MR wagons 108599 and 77168 on 3rd and 27th May 1899 from Cartwright Colliery, Swadlincote to Porthywaen on account of 'The Coal Miners Co-op Brotherhood'. It would be interesting to know more about this organisation.

Stone, Salt and Tank Wagons

Probably the first products carried in tank wagons on to the Cambrian would have been lamp oil and creosote. With the invention of the motor car petroleum spirit became an important traffic. The first tank wagons had 'D' shaped tanks (see MRN May 1960) but by the late 1880s cylindrical tanks began to appear. Tar, however, was carried in rectangular tanks.

Unfortunately I have been unable to discover any information on tank wagons which worked on to the Cambrian other than a photograph in *Cambrian Railways Album Vol.2* p37 [4] which shows an United Alkali Company's tank wagon in a train at Portmadoc in 1925. In post grouping days tank wagons belonging to Anglo-American Oil Co. and Shell Mex worked on to the Cambrian section since the two companies had depots at Oswestry by 1922. Later Anglo-American and National Benzole had depots at Aberystwyth.

Salt was another product which arrived in PO wagons. With the Northwich salt works close to the Cambrian system no doubt most salt came from there, but the only load I have been able to trace is a load from the Salt Union, Stoke Works in wagon No.268 to Llynclys.

For those interested there is a comprehensive article entitled 'Wagons of the Salt Union Limited' in *Modellers' BackTrack*.[40] This contains plenty of drawings and photographs.

Sometimes stone was carried from the Chirk Castle Lime Works, invoicing station Llangollen Road, to Llynclys for Salop County Council in GW wagons. The delivery of stone from Ceiriog Granite and Chirk Castle Works wagons to Llynclys might be considered as a case of taking coals to Newcastle with the Porthywaen quarries nearby. However, they were consigned to Salop County Council and were probably part of a contract covering other delivery points. It is perhaps worth recording that one of the shortest journeys made by a Porthywaen Lime Co. wagon was from Porthywaen to Llynclys, a distance of about 1¼ miles! That was also for the Salop County Council.

Wagon Routing ....

It is worth considering some of the routes taken by PO wagons entering and leaving Cambrian territory. Route lists were issued by the various railway companies which laid down the routes to be followed by parcels, goods, mineral and live stock traffic unless it was otherwise specially consigned. Unfortunately the only information I have of such lists are four pages from the Cambrian June 1879 edition which covers the LNWR, MR and LSWR, so I have had to rely on other sources such as goods invoices and wagon labels. The delivery of coal from the North Staffordshire coalfield was straight-forward being sent via Crewe and Whitchurch.

.... from North Wales ....

The transportation of coal from North Wales was more competitive after the opening of the Wrexham and Ellesmere Railway, particularly as some of the collieries were connected to both the GWR and the Wrexham, Mold and Connah's Quay Railway. Wagon invoices for loads from Broughton and Plas Power, New Broughton and Vron collieries show that they were then sent via Wrexham and Ellesmere. The Cambrian issued circulars _(transcribed opposite)_ instructing staff to get all traffic from some ten collieries with which the WM&CQR had access routed via Ellesmere and all open wagons to be returned via that route unless otherwise ordered. The distance to Wrexham via Ellesmere from Oswestry was about 20 miles whereas the direct route via Gobowen was just over 14½ miles.

.... and from South Wales

Coal from collieries in the east of the South Wales coalfield was routed by Merthyr and Talyllyn. Traffic from the coalfield to the north of Swansea used either the Neath & Brecon Railway to Brecon and on to Talyllyn, or the LNWR Central Wales line to Builth Road. Exceptions have been recorded, however.

On 31st October 1899 a wagon carrying 10t 4cwt of anthracite to Porthywaen from New Cawdor Colliery, Garnant was routed over the GWR via Llanelly to Pencader, then via the Manchester and Milford to Aberystwyth, finally completing its journey over the Cambrian. A few months later seven wagons carrying a total of 70t 3cwt of anthracite to Porthywaen were dispatched via Llandovery and Builth Road, a much shorter route.

Lest the former be thought a mistake I have a record of other wagons following the same route. However there may have been a query, as a memo in November 1899 from the Cambrian District Traffic Agent, Cardiff to Mr Carsley, stationmaster at Llynclys, enquires "as to the route of wagons from Pantyffynnon and Garnant to Porthywaen." Unfortunately the reply is not available but traffic was still being sent via the longer route in 1900.

Outbound Wagons

The routes taken by mineral traffic from the Cambrian have not been so easy to establish. Fortunately, a few Cambrian mineral invoices from Minffordd have survived from 1917. Before looking at these it is interesting to note that if the product being transported was from the Pwllheli Granite Co. the invoice originating station was given as 'Minffordd', but if the load was slate brought down on the Festiniog Railway the originating station was given as 'Minffordd for Blaenau Festiniog'.

On 22nd February 1917 four wagons of macadam were dispatched in Pwllheli Granite Co. wagons to Capenhurst for R Pardoe, Surveyor, Heswall, via Dolgelley. A single Pwllheli Granite Co. wagon carrying chippings sent on 24th of the same month was sent to Burrows Lodge, Swansea for R Heath, Surveyor, Swansea. This load was routed via Talyllyn and Merthyr whereas Brecon and the N&BR route might have been more obvious.

Into Decline

The heyday of the private owner was prior to World War I; afterwards a slow decline set in through a change from coal to oil, particularly for shipping and large manufacturing concerns and because of amalgamation, particularly of colliery companies, until finally, at the outbreak of World War II the Government requisitioned all PO wagons with the exception of those used for certain types of traffic. Among those were Steetley Lime Co. and BQC, Llanelwedd; such wagons were lettered NON-POOL in white.

Finally ....

It should be noted that many of the wagons shown as invoiced to Llynclys in the Appendix were, in fact, intended for the Porthywaen Lime Co. at Porthywaen.

CAMBRIAN RAILWAYS COMPANY.

GOODS SUPERINTENDENT'S OFFICE.

Cir. No. 100   OSWESTRY, NOV. 4th, 1895
R.

Coal from Wrexham District.

The W. M. and C. Q. Co. have access to the undermentioned Collieries, and now that the Wrexham and Ellesmere Line is opened, please get all traffic possible consigned via Ellesmere.

Empty Wagons consigned to any of these Collieries must be sent to W. M. and C. Q. Co., via Ellesmere, unless otherwise ordered.

Wrexham and Acton.	Brynmally.
Gatewen.	Gwersyllt.
New Broughton.	Ffrwd.
Plaspower.	Brymbo.
Westminster.	Vron.

Please note and acknowledge receipt.

J. SHEPHERD.

CAMBRIAN CIRCULARS WITH INSTRUCTIONS FOR ROUTING OF COAL TRAFFIC

CAMBRIAN RAILWAYS COMPANY.

GOODS MANAGER'S OFFICE.
OSWESTRY, JANUARY 3RD, 1896

Circular No. 103

Coal Traffic — Wrexham Collieries to Cambrian Stations.

With reference to my Circular 100 of Nov. 4th you will please endeavour to induce Coal Merchants and others receiving at your station coal from the Collieries therein named to order it to be sent via Wrexham and Ellesmere.

Acknowledge receipt on form at foot.

W. FINCHETT.
GOODS MANAGER

31

Chapter 5

Directory of Foreign Traders on the Cambrian

Barton & Co. *(Plate 22)*

An 1886 directory lists Thomas B Barton as a salt, lime and coal merchant at the goods station and 26 Home Market, Wrexham. By 1892 he is listed only as a coal merchant at 13 Temple Row. A directory of 1907 still lists T B Barton but a wagon in a photograph dated 1906 and lettered 'Barton & Co.' also has the address of '13 Temple Row' which rather implies that T B Barton had formed a company.

This is confirmed by the 1913/14 directory which lists Barton & Co., 13 Temple Row. The RCH Handbook for 1926 lists the firm as Barton & Co. (Coal) Ltd. The company was still in existence in the mid-1930s and probably longer.

There is a blue and white enamel plate in existence lettered 'Barton & Co./ When empty return to / Ford Green, / N.S.R.'

So obviously the company obtained their coal not only from North Wales.

Bignall Hill Colliery

This colliery was owned by J R Wedgwood, or the representative of the late J R Wedgwood from 1869 until 22nd December 1927 when it became the subsidiary of Settle Speakman. The colliery also operated coke ovens and ran coke wagons.

Drg: MRN Jul 1974 p344.

Photo: Shropshire Records & Research Unit. (48)

H Billington Ltd. *(Figure 19)*

The 1892 Chester Directory lists the firm as Coal & Lime Merchants but, when the 1905/6 edition was published, lime had been dropped from the description. After several moves the 1958 address is given as Black Diamond St., a most appropriate address! The firm was still listed as late as 1967 but does not appear in the 1970 directory so presumably it was out of business by then.

A photograph of Whitfield Colliery about 1905 dimly shows a J H Billington wagon on the end of which may be seen the letters 'J H B' spread over two planks with the 'H' between the end stanchions.

Black Park Colliery *(Plates 23 and 24)*

This colliery was situated just north of Chirk and was served by a branch from the Shrewsbury to Chester railway line and was one of the oldest collieries in North Wales, dating back to Elizabeth I.

Originally the coal was mined by a series of pits but in 1805 the workings were leased by T E Ward who set about developing the site. At this time the workings were served by a tramway which ran down to a dock on the Ellesmere Canal. By 1860 John Stott Milne and Co. were the owners but in 1877 a company was formed which took over the mine and improved it. The colliery produced household, manufacturing and steam coals and closed in 1949.

Plate 22 - Barton & Co., Wrexham

Built by Gloucester RC&W Co. Perhaps the most interesting thing about this wagon is its body colour described as 'chocolate'. This has caused much discussion amongst modellers over the years, suggestions being made that the colour of chocolate has changed over the last 90 years. Perhaps it has; a Chambers Twentieth Century Dictionary of 1901 describes the colour as 'dark reddish-brown' whereas 'The Oxford Reference Dictionary' of 1987 describes it as 'dark brown' colour. If it is of any interest to intending modellers I am painting my model with Humbrol 'Hull-red' No.177.

M Lloyd collection

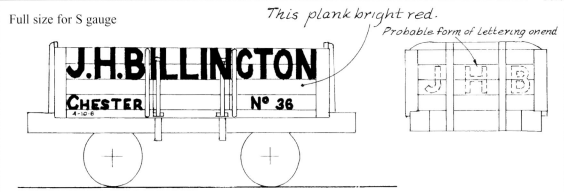

Full size for S gauge

This plank bright red.

Probable form of Lettering on end

J.H.BILLINGTON

CHESTER   Nº 36

4-10-6

JHB

Figure 19

Livery:- Grey, centre plank bright red. Lettering white shaded black.
Running gear and strapping black.
Sources: 'Shropshire Magazine' photograph 1972. Livery, H.B. Holland

William Blake (Hereford)

This firm makes its first appearance in the Hereford Directory in 1917 with its office at 9 West St., Hereford. The 1914 edition lists the South Wales Coal Company at the same address while a guide to Hereford, circa 1922, contains a whole-page advert shared by both firms. Wm. Blake and Sons Ltd. are shown as the proprietors of the South Wales Coal Co., while Blake's managing director is given as J H Blake.

The company was still in business in the early 1970s.

The SWC Co. advertises the supply of coal, coke, lime and salt while Blakes are wholesale Coal and Coke Factors and Merchants and proprietors of a number of small firms at stations in Herefordshire and Shropshire. Besides its wagons being recorded in Oswestry a good photograph of one at West Bromwich in 1934 appears in *Road Vehicles of the Great Western Railway* p.79. [19]

Plate 23 - Black Park Colliery, Ruabon

Built by the Ince Wagon & Ironworks Co. Ltd. Although Chirk might seem a more accurate description of its location, the sorting sidings would have been at Ruabon. The livery is quite complicated. The basic colour was red-oxide, lettering white, the top line of which appears to be shaded black. The ironwork black but on the door there is a white oval with a crimson 'hand'.

Courtesy H B Holland

Plate 24 - Black Park Colliery, Ruabon

A photograph of a southbound train at Four Crosses. The Black Park Colliery wagons are lettered in the earlier and smaller style. Note that the number is on the door and the crimson 'hand' on the wagon side. Unfortunately the second wagon is obscured but it looks as if the white oval has a black edging.

M Lloyd collection

Breconshire Coal & Lime Co.

This company had depots at Builth Wells and Llanidloes. It seems to have undergone a financial re-organisation in 1923 as the RCH Handbook for 1926 gives the title as Breconshire Coal & Lime Co. (1923) Ltd. There was a fine blue enamel sign bearing the company's name in Lion Place, Brecon but it disappeared sometime before the redevelopment of the area.

Brereton Colliery

Situated between Hednesford and Rugeley Town (LNWR).

Broughton & Plas Power Colliery Co. _(Plates 25/26)_

Plas Power Colliery, which opened in 1877, was acquired by the owners of the Old Broughton Colliery when it flooded in 1878. The year 1881 saw the formation of the Broughton & Plas Power Colliery Co., which also owned the Gatewen Colliery which closed in 1932. In the early 1900s the B & PPC Co. took over the Vron Colliery which was approached by a steeply graded branch line from Brymbo station on the WM&CQR. Bersham Colliery, which was sunk about 1870, was

bought in 1910 by the B&PPC Co. who developed it. The colliery had a connection on the Down side of the GWR main line, about a mile south of Rhos Junction, but closed in December 1986.

Plas Power Colliery had connections to both the WM&CQR and GWR lines which ran near to one another on their way to Brymbo. The colliery closed in July 1938.

Gatewen Colliery was serviced by sidings connected to the WM&CQR Brymbo branch and to the GWR Moss Valley line.

Plas Power and Gatewen Collieries produced coking, gas, household, manufacturing and steam coals; Bersham produced the same with the exception of coking coal. Steam coal was mined at Vron Colliery.

Brynkinalt Colliery _(Plate 27)_

Just to the north of Chirk, to the east of the GWR line was situated Brynkinalt Colliery, opened about 1870. Mr William Y Craig bought the colliery in 1893. Craig also owned mines in North Staffordshire and became the first manager of the Midland Coal, Coke & Iron Co. in 1890. He represented North Staffs in Parliament from 1880 to 1885.

In 1913 he re-opened the closed Ifton Rhyn Colliery about two miles away from Brynkinalt. This was then known as Ifton Colliery. Later, probably in the early 1920s, Brynkinalt was closed although the shaft was used for ventilating Ifton Colliery which closed in 1968.

Brynkinalt produced household, manufacturing and steam coal while household and steam coals came from Ifton.

Ceiriog Granite Co. _(Plate 28)_

The Ceiriog Granite Co. worked Hendre Quarry which was about 1³/₄ miles above Glyn Ceiriog and commenced production in 1875. Until the advent of the motor lorry in the 1920s, its output was

---

Plate 25 (upper) - Broughton & Plas Power Collieries

Another 'chocolate' wagon built by the Gloucester RC&W Co. in 1899 and registered by the GWR. This company's wagons were to be found all over North Wales in places such as Blaenau Ffestiniog and Nantlle.

Plate 26 (lower) - Vron Colliery, near Brymbo

Reconstructed by the Gloucester RC&W Co. in May 1898, the livery of this wagon is shown as purple-brown, lettering white shaded black

Courtesy HMRS

transported over the Glyn Valley Tramway to Chirk where most of it was transferred to standard gauge wagons although some went into canal barges.

The Ceiriog Granite Co. was absorbed into the British Quarrying Co. in 1929 and the quarry closed in 1950.

Besides using its own standard gauge wagons it also made use of GWR wagons. The company owned narrow-gauge wagons as well as standard-gauge ones.

Chatterley-Whitfield Collieries Ltd. *(Plate 29)*

Chatterley-Whitfield was one of the largest mining companies in the North Staffordshire coalfield owning collieries in the Tunstall area. It had originated as the Whitfield Colliery Company but after merging with the Chatterley Iron Company it assumed the name by which it is best known. After the merger the iron works were closed.

Photo: MRC Mar 1970 p69 and notes.

Plate 27 - W Y Craig & Sons Ltd., Ruabon

The wagon on the left shows the style of lettering when Brynkinalt Colliery was working. After the closure of that colliery and working was confined to Ifton, the style on the right-hand wagon was adopted.

Courtesy R Carpenter

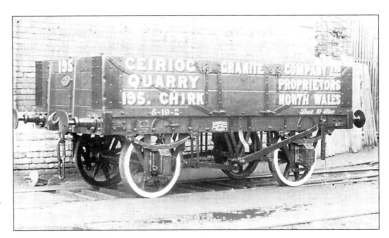

Plate 28 - Ceiriog Granite Co., Chirk

Built by Charles Roberts & Co. Livery was probably chocolate with black ironwork. The lettering was white, shaded black. Possibly the body colour was changed to medium grey in the late 1920s.

Courtesy HMRS

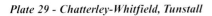

Plate 29 - Chatterley-Whitfield, Tunstall

Built by Hurst Nelson and registered by the NSR. Livery was grey, lettering white and shaded black where shown. All ironwork was black. The monogram on the door was not always carried.

Courtesy HMRS

Chirk Castle Lime Works

These works were reached by a siding off the Down side of the GW main line, just north of Whitehurst Halt, which ran as far as Froncysyllte where there were extensive quarries and lime kilns served by narrow gauge tramways.

I have found no clear photograph of Chirk Castle Lime wagons but in a distant view the name can be seen on the top two planks of a 5-plank open wagon. Two wagon labels for loads to Llynclys give wagon numbers 18 c.c. and 21 c.c.

Frederic Chubb *(Plate 30)*

In an 1870 trade directory Frederic Chubb is listed as a stone merchant and quarry owner. By 1900 he is listed under coal merchants having premises at Abbey Foregate wharf and railway goods yard and wharves, Old Coleham.

Evans & Bevan *(Plate 32)*

A long established company existing probably from the 1880s until nationalisation; their wagons were photographed in 1940. In 1907 the company was operating Brynteg (closed 1954) and Seven Sisters (closed 1963). By 1924 Onllwyn Nos 1, 2

and 3 were being worked by Evans & Bevan; previously the proprietor had been Sir Griffith Thomas, who also owned Maesymarchog Colliery. All those collieries produced anthracite.

Onllwyn No.3 closed in 1962 and Onllwyn No.1 closed 1964.

Drg: MRN Jun 1939 (7p open)
        MRN Dec 1944 (6p open)
Photo: MRN Jun 1939 (7p open)

Ffrith Colliery Company

Although the invoicing station for this colliery was Llanfynydd in 1907, it was situated just south of Ffrith on the Brymbo to Mold branch.

Coal was first produced there in 1872 and it was known as Mr Charlwood's Colliery. By 1901 it was owned by the Ffrith Coal & Fireclay Co. After an apparent closure, it was reopened in 1914 by the Brynmally Colliery Co. and called Glascoed Colliery but it finally closed in 1922.

Florence Coal & Iron Co. Ltd. *(Plate 31)*

The Duke of Sutherland started this colliery in 1874. It was situated at Longton, Stoke-on-Trent and was reached by a private line 2¹/₂ miles long from Trentham. Following a short closure in 1895, new shafts were sunk.

The company became a subsidiary of Shelton Iron, Steel & Coal Co. Ltd. from 1911.

Drg: MRC Mar 1970.
Photo: MRC Mar 1970.
Photo: L&GRP 3804 - Dumb buffer wagon.

Plate 30 - Frederic Chubb

A wagon with a rather angular style of lettering which seems to have been used over a long period. A photograph of Kerry taken in 1904 shows a dumb buffer wagon with the same style of lettering. The livery is not known.

Courtesy P Matthews

Plate 31 - Florence Coal & Iron Co. Ltd. & Glebe Colly.

A goods train heading south at Llanymynech c.1904; note the Cambrian cattle and 8T dropside wagons. The Florence Co. wagon is pre-RCH 1887 specification and is fitted with dumb-buffers and wooden brake shoes. Livery was a dark grey which faded in service and usually the ironwork was black. Lettering was white often with black shading.

The small lettering in the LH corner reads 'Empty to Trentham N.S.R.' The Glebe Colliery wagon is of much more modern construction and its livery is believed to be black with white lettering. The diamond encompassed John Challinor & Co Ltd., the owner of the colliery.

Courtesy L&GRP

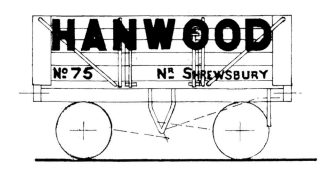

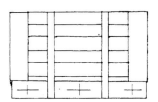

No 75   NR SHREWSBURY

Source:- Photograph. Assumed dimensions

Livery:- Probably light grey
body, black ironwork,
white lettering.

Figure 20

Full size for S gauge

Foxfield Colliery

This colliery was situated at Dilhorne, near Cheadle. It was connected to the NSR by a private line 3 1/2 miles long, now operated by a preservation company. The shafts were sunk in the 1880s by John and Enoch Mann of Blakely House, Cresswellford.

In 1893 the Mann Brothers formed a private limited company known as the Foxfield Colliery Co. Ltd.

Following voluntary liquidation in 1927 the colliery was acquired by the nearby Parkhall Colliery Co. Ltd. and the company became known as Parkhall and Foxfield until 1936. It then became the Foxfield Colliery Ltd, Parkhall having closed in 1930. Foxfield closed in 1965.

Glebe Colliery *(Plate 31)*

This colliery, situated in Fenton, Stoke-on-Trent, was owned by John Challinor & Co. until 1900

when it was acquired by John Heath & Co. Ltd.

In 1910 it became the Fenton Collieries Ltd. and in 1930 became a subsidiary of Settle Speakman & Co. Ltd.

Drg: MRN   Jul 1974,
Glebe and Fenton Collieries wagon.
Photo: L&GRP 3804.

Hanwood Colliery *(Figure 20)*

Hanwood Colliery was situated about four miles south west of Shrewsbury and was served by a branch on the Down side of the Shrewsbury to Welshpool line. The colliery commenced operation in the 1870s. Hanwood and Moat Hall Collieries (Salop) Ltd. was formed in 1921.

Its coal was popular in Central Wales and as far as the coast and it was not unknown in South Wales.

However, it was apparently not highly rated in Shrewsbury!

Plate 32 - Evans & Bevan, Neath

A view taken at Seven Sisters Colliery in the early 1920s. The figure on the left is Dai James, that font of knowledge on the N&BR. The other figure is the redoubtable Colonel Bevan. Livery was a very dark grey, almost black, lettering white, perhaps shaded red, except for the smaller lettering. The two hearts are red, bordered white.

Courtesy Dai James

Joseph Hawkins & Sons Ltd.

This firm operated Cannock Old Coppice Colliery situated at Wyrley and Cheslyn just south of Cannock. The RCH Handbook for 1926 gives the firm's title as T A Hawkins and Sons Ltd.

Drg: _MRC May 1959 p108 - 12T 7-plank open showing a later style of lettering._

Photo: _'Celebration of Steam, North Wales' p23._

Highley Mining Co.

Formed in the 1870s, the Highley Mining Co. was situated on the Severn Valley branch of the GWR. In 1907, besides the colliery at Highley, the company also owned Kinlet Colliery which opened in the 1890s and closed in 1937. In 1915 the company bought Billingsley Colliery which closed in 1921 during the miners' strike.

Highley Colliery, which closed in 1968, was serviced by a short branch up an incline at Highley station while Kidnet and Billingsley were served by a branch line about three miles long from a junction with the SVR about a mile south of Highley. All three collieries produced household, manufacturing and steam coal.

Hollybush Colliery (Plate 33)

This colliery was started by E D Williams, one time High Sheriff of Monmouthshire, in 1888 and when he died it was taken over by Trustees. The colliery closed in 1921. The colliery was unusual in that while the coal was brought up the shaft, the miners reached the coal-face via a drift.

A Gloucester RC&W Co. photograph of one of the colliery's wagons announced that it produced house, gas and smith's coal.

Plate 33 - Hollybush Colliery, near Newport

Livery black with white lettering.

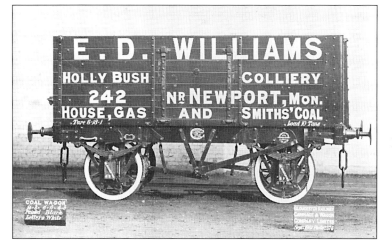

James & Emanuel

66 Dock Street, Newport in 1907;

90 Dock Street, Newport in 1923 & 1933.

A wagon label headed 'Western Valleys, Millbrook' used in 1918, describes the company as Colliery Proprietors. The GWR List of Collieries 1907 shows that they were working Llandavel Colliery at Aberbeeg while the proprietor of Millbrook Colliery, Crumlin Low Level, is given as Millbrook Colliery Co. Neither Llandavel nor James & Emanuel are shown in the 1924 list but the latter is included in the 1926 and 1933 RCH Handbooks.

Millbrook Colliery is included in the 1924 list, the postal address being given as 90 Dock St. The output of Millbrook Colliery was household coal.

Lilleshall Co. Ltd. (See plate 16)

A long-established company dealing in coal, lime and engineering products. Its lime production moved to Nantmawr when the quarries became flooded. The Lilleshall Co. also had several pits in the triangle formed by the railway lines from Wellington to Shifnal and Newport, Donington Colliery being one of them. The company had contracts to supply coal to the Cambrian, GW and LNW railways.

The wagon label for the colliery spells the name as shown above but the 1904 OS 1-inch map and the RCH Handbook of Stations shows the name spelt 'Donnington'.

Madeley Wood Colliery Co.

Sometimes known as the Madeley Wood Co., this was an old firm. In later years it operated Kemberton Colliery, producing gas, household, manufacturing and steam coals. Madeley Wood closed in 1967.

A coal price ledger for 1932-1938 shows that it supplied coal to a large part of Cambrian territory via merchants. For instance, the CWS supplied coal from the colliery to Oswestry, Aberystwyth and Machynlleth, while P H Breeze of Shrewsbury supplied the "Welsh coast from Towyn up to Pwllheli and including the district near the north coast of the Cambrian Rly. Line from Welshpool to Aberystwyth".

Midland Coal, Coke & Iron Co. Ltd.

This large firm had several pits and an ironworks in Apedale served by the NSR but closed about 1930.

Drg: _'Coal Trade Wagons' pp22/23._

Photo: _MRC Oct 1969 pp305/6._

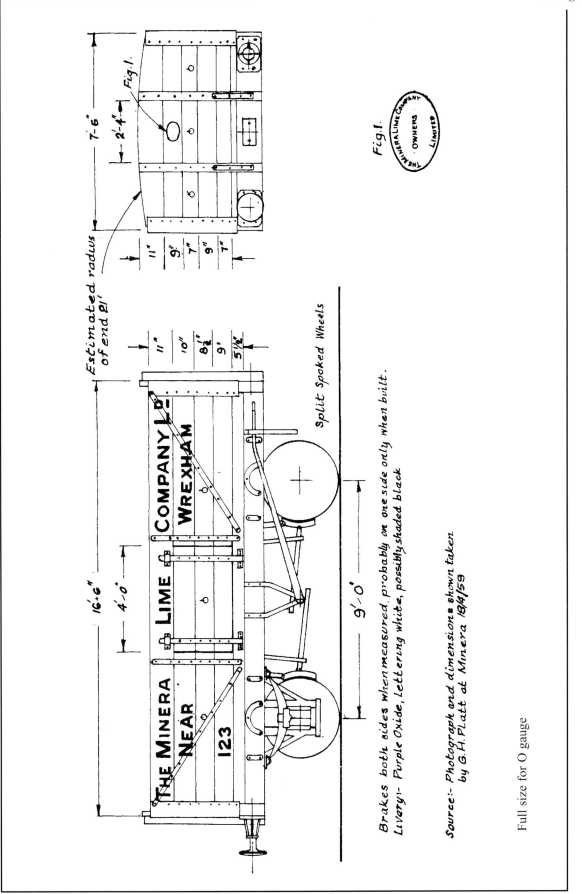

Figure 21

Full size for O gauge

Minera Lime Co. *(Figure 21 and Plate 34)*

The company was formed in 1852, one of its directors being Henry Robinson who was much involved in railways and coal mining in the Wrexham area. In 1899 the company took over Lester's Quarry. A large amount of the quarry's output went to chemical works in Cheshire and Lancashire but most went to the nearby Brymbo Steelworks.

The company was taken over by Adam Lythgoe in 1954 but in 1967 Tarmac Roadstone Holdings took control. The Quarry closed about 1994.

The company had a large number of railway wagons and as far as I have been able to ascertain these were all opens, the contents being covered by sheets. For an interesting history of the Minera quarries and mines see bibliography.

Mossfield Colliery Ltd.

This colliery had its beginnings in 1850 when it was owned by Hawley and Bridgwood. Following an explosion in 1889 the colliery was acquired by Wm. Rigby & Co. in 1892. In 1902 the Mossfield Colliery Company Ltd. was formed, becoming a subsidiary of Settle Speakman Ltd. in 1927.

Mynydd Maen Colliery Co.

This colliery was situated on a branch from Trosnant Junction, which ran parallel with the Taff Vale Extension line through Pontypool, Clarence St. The junction itself was on the Eastern Valleys line. Although not mentioned in the 1907 GWR List of Collieries, it does appear in the 1924 list. Its output is given as household coal.

Also listed under the company's name is Wern Hill Colliery, output coking, gas, manufacturing and steam coals. A siding left the Eastern Valleys line just to the north of Crane Street to serve the colliery, which was situated on the east side of the line. It would appear that Wern Hill was the older of the two collieries as it is listed in the 1907 list, the proprietor being D Roberts.

Ref: A view of a Mynydd Maen wagon appears in a photograph of MWR station building at Talyllyn Junction. F Moore's photograph.

New Haden Collieries

New Haden Collieries were situated on the Cheadle branch of the NSR and were sunk in the mid-19th century. The colliery had several ownerships and eventually closed in 1943.

For a detailed and interesting account see *The Cheadle Collieries and their Railways.* [12]

Old Radnor Trading Company *(Figures 22-24)*

This company originated as the 'Old Radnor Coal, Lime, Roadstone and General Trading Co. Ltd.' in August 1875. The shorter title was adopted in 1901 and the 'O R T Co.' style was probably introduced during World War I. It had extensive quarries and lime kilns at Dolyhir on the New Radnor branch and, at one period, owned 240 wagons.

In its early years the company had lime wagons with a 'cottage' roof, a photograph of Dolyhir lime kiln shows a dumb buffer example. Besides dealing in coal and lime, the company also handled coke and building materials such as slate, bricks and pipes. At one time it had depots at 26 different stations.

The quarries are now worked by Nash Rocks and have been road-served for a long time. The former offices of the company in Kington are used by the Public Library, the company's monogram being etched into the glass of the window.

Plate 34 - Minera Lime Co., near Wrexham

A smaller and earlier wagon than the one measured by Geoff Platt and shown in the drawing. 'Wrexham' appears to have been freshly painted!

Courtesy J P Richards

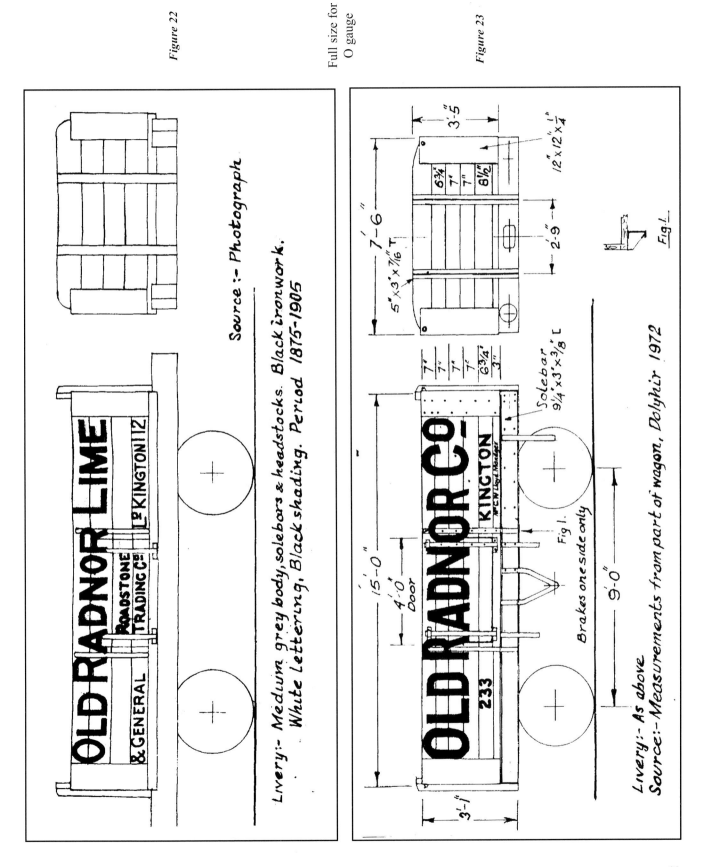

Figure 22

Source :- Photograph

Livery :- Medium grey body, solebars & headstocks. Black ironwork.
White lettering, Black shading. Period 1875-1905

OLD RADNOR LIME
& GENERAL
ROADSTONE TRADING CO.
L.D. KINGTON 112

Full size for O gauge

Figure 23

3'-5"
7'-6"
5" x 3" x 7/16" T
6¾"
7"
7"
8½"
2'-9"
12" x 12" x 1/4"

Fig I.

15'-0"
4'-0"
Door
9'-0"
3'-1"

7"
7"
7"
7"
6¾"
3"
Solebar
9¼" x 3" x 3/8" L

OLD RADNOR CO.
KINGTON
Mr C.W. Lloyd, Manager
233

Fig I.
Brakes one side only

Livery :- As above
Source :- Measurements from part of wagon, Dolyhir 1972

41

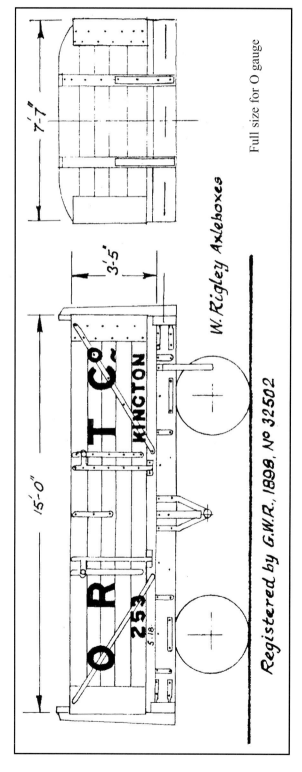

Figure 24

W. Rigley Axleboxes

Registered by G.W.R., 1898, Nº 32502

Full size for O gauge

7'-7"

15'-0"

3'-5"

O R T Cº

KINGTON

253

5/18

Powell Duffryn Steam Coal Co. Ltd.

This company was formed in 1864 and by 1880 it controlled 13 collieries. According to the GWR 1923 List of Collieries this had risen to 16. Unfortunately the two labels I have for loads to Llynclys do not state from which colliery they originated.

Drg: *MRN Apr 1960 - 10T 6-plank open with dumb buffers.*

The Radnorshire Coal, Lime & General Supply Co.

A 1905 directory shows the above company as having a depot at Doldowlod while an advertisement in an 1880 directory states that there were depots on the Knighton and Central Wales Railway.

The company's offices were situated at Knighton.

Ruabon Coal & Coke Co. Ltd. *(Figure 25)*

This company, originally known as the Ruabon Coal Co., was formed in 1856 by Great Western Railway officers and their friends, Sir David Gooch being chairman. The object was to carry large quantities of coal over the GWR and with this in mind an agreement was made between the railway and the coal company whereby the latter undertook to send such a quantity of coal for more than 100 miles that would produce a gross revenue of £40,000 pa.

The Ruabon Coal Co. took over the Ruabon Colliery owned by Henry Robinson, an engineer and entrepreneur who was born in Banff in 1816 and moved to the Wrexham area in 1842.

The Company operated several pits known as the 'Brandie Pits'. These pits were situated to the west of Johnstown and when they became flooded the company decided to sink a new pit just to the east of the Wrexham-Ruabon railway line.

This pit became known as Hafod Colliery, serviced by a connection to the GWR main line, and produced its first coal in 1867.

It produced coking, household, manufacturing and steam coals.

Around 1880 the Ruabon Coal Co. went into liquidation and a new company, the Ruabon Coal & Coke Co. Ltd. purchased the colliery. In 1933 ownership passed to the Carlton Main Colliery Co. Ltd. who earlier had taken over Llay Main Colliery but the name Ruabon Coal & Coke Co. Ltd. was retained.

Hafod Colliery closed in 1968.

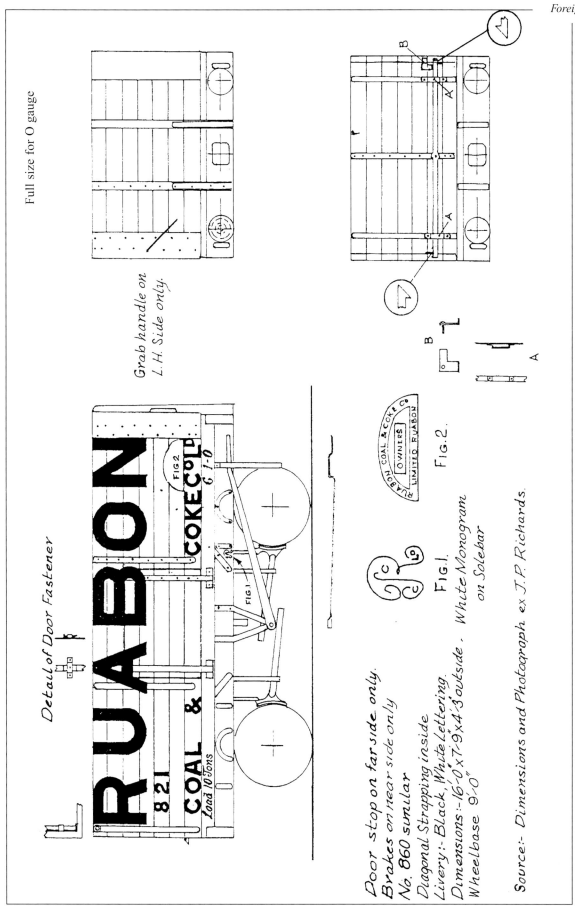

Figure 25

The Salt Union

The Salt Union was formed in 1888 and absorbed a large number of firms mostly in Cheshire but included the Stoke Prior works in Worcestershire. A history of the Union accompanied by drawings and photographs may be found in *Modellers' Back Track*, Feb/Mar 1994 Vol.3 No.6.

Settle Speakman

This company took over some of the North Staffs collieries that supplied coal and coke to the Cambrian area. Among the companies taken over were Glebe and Bignall Hill Collieries.

Drg: *MRN Jul 1974 - and detailed history of the company.*

Photos: MRN Jul 1974.

Shelton Iron, Steel & Coal Co. Ltd.

The predecessors of this company date back as far as at least 1819 when the pits were sunk to provide coal for the iron works. The Racecourse Pits at Shelton were opened in 1870 and lasted until 1937.

Deep Pit, Hanley commenced operation in 1854 and closed in 1962. Silverdale Colliery was acquired at some date.

The Shelton Co. also had an interest in the Florence Colliery and Hem Heath Colliery at Trentham.

Photo: MRC Mar 1970 p68.

Sneyd Colliery Company

The Sneyd Colliery Company, Burslem, was formed in the early 1880s to re-open a pit which had been flooded after closure in the late 1860s.

Sneyd Colliery supplied coal to numerous merchants on the Cambrian system, even as far as Minffordd.

Henry Sowter

Sowter's yard was on the bed of an old canal at Newcastle, Staffordshire, and entry was under a low bridge necessitating some low wagons. He probably acted as a coal factor as well as a merchant. On the occasion of one of his wagon's visit to Llynclys it delivered a 5t 10cwt load of breeze.

Drg: *MRC Aug 1970.*

H Stothart & Co.

This firm was a coal factor or shipper, the office being at 43 James St., Cardiff Docks.

Photo: MRN Sep 1970 p500.

Talk-o'-th'- Hill Colliery Co. Ltd.

One of the more unusual colliery company names! The colliery was situated at the end of a branch from Chatterley Junction and was one of the oldest collieries in the North Staffordshire coalfield. The colliery also had coke ovens. It was acquired by the Shelton Iron, Steel & Coal Co. by 1923 and was closed in 1928.

Drg: *MRN Dec 1969 p628.*

Photo: MRC Jul 1970 p219.

Thomas & Co., Swansea

This company's letter heading describes themselves as 'Shippers of the Big and Peacock Vein Anthracite Coal' with collieries at Abercrave and Gurnos, the office address being 13 Cambrian Place, Swansea.

However, I have been unable to trace any collieries belonging to the firm at either location, but there are numerous invoices for loads from the New Cawdor Colliery, Garnant and New Cwmgorse Colliery, Gwaun-Cae-Gurwen!

The company seems to have owned a large number

Plate 35 - Vauxhall Colliery, Ruabon

Built Hurst Nelson and registered by the GWR in 1903. Its livery was probably red-oxide with white lettering shaded black.

Courtesy HMRS

of wagons, as a memo from W Finchett, Goods Manager of the Cambrian to Mr Carsley, the Agent at Llynclys says "....that 33 of their wagons are under load with the Porthywaen Coy. and that they only have a few on hand."

The memo ends "I understand you have been asked for the information, please see that it is sent without delay."

Vauxhall Colliery *(Plate 35)*

The pit was sunk in the late 1850s and was situated on the west side of the GWR line between Ruabon and Johnstown. Originally known as Kenyon Colliery, it appears to have changed its name to Vauxhall in the 1860s when a new pit was sunk. After a warning of closure in 1925 the colliery finally closed in 1928. The mine produced gas, household and steam coals.

Westminster Colliery Co. *(Plate 36)*

The Westminster Colliery, which worked several pits in the Moss Valley near Wrexham, had its origins in the eighteenth century. In 1887 the Westminster Colliery Company acquired Gwersyllt Colliery which had been sunk in 1862. The Westminster used this colliery mainly for pumping purposes.

By 1925, when the Westminster Colliery closed, its owners were then the Westminster Brymbo Coal and Coke Company. Both these collieries produced gas, heating, manufacturing and steam coals.

Drg: 'Coal Trade Wagons' p13 - Dumb buffer wagon.

The Wigan Coal & Iron Co.

This company dates from 1865 when a number of mining concerns in the Wigan area amalgamated. *Modellers' BackTrack* for Feb/Mar 1995, Vol.4,

No.6 has a history of the company which contains drawings and photographs of their wagons.

Although I have only one record of the company's wagons on the Cambrian (at Portmadoc), their wagons ranged all over North Wales and no doubt were to be seen at other Cambrian stations.

Richard Williams & Sons Ltd.

A coal factor with offices in Liverpool who would appear to have a large number of wagons as No.423 can be seen in a photograph taken at Aberdovey circa 1911.

A 5-plank dumb-buffered wagon No.134 appears in a photograph of Llanfihangel station.

Photo: Nat Library of Wales C.39.

Wynnstay Colliery

This colliery, sunk in 1856, was owned by the New British Iron Co., Acrefair. The pit was sandwiched between the GWR line just south of Ruabon station and the main road which became the A483.

The colliery was served by a connection from the Plas Madoc branch which crossed the GW line by a high bridge. Its output was gas, household and steam coals.

The *GWR Magazine* for 1929 carries a photograph and short article on the demolition of this bridge on pages 446/7. The pit closed in July 1927.

The colliery had the distinction of being the only Denbighshire colliery visited by Royalty. This visit took place in 1889 when Prince Henry of Battenburg and Princess Alice descended the Green Pit of the colliery.

Drg: MRN Nov 1969 - 10T 5-plank open.

Plate 36 - Westminster Colliery, Wrexham

This example was built by the Gloucester RC&W Co. around 1865. It was possibly painted red-oxide with black strapping and white lettering. Note the GWR register plate between the 'V' hanger, the number being 2073.

Courtesy HMRS

Chapter 6

Wagon Label Notes and Illustrations

Nearly all the collieries and quarries mentioned in the text had their own labels but an exception seems to be Hanwood Colliery which used a GWR label. The labels were carried in label holders on the sides of the wagons or on solebars. If no holder was provided then the label was pinned to the side of the wagon.

Of the ones illustrated the colour was mostly buff with black printing, the Staffordshire Knot on the Florence Coal & Iron Co. was red. The Chirk Castle Lime Works labels were yellow, while those of the Ceiriog Granite Co. were off-white, Black Park Colliery used pale green labels. "Urgent" on the Westminster Colliery example was in red and on the reverse was

"Empty to Westminster Colliery Wrexham Date   ".

The small but interesting museum at Montgomery has a Savin & Co. wagon label in its display of railway artefacts.

When the labels were removed from wagons they were impaled on $1/8$in diameter wire about 13in long and turned up at one end, the other protruded from a polished wooden handle shaped like a darning mushroom.

FROM
CHIRK CASTLE LIME WORKS.

To *Llynclys Station*

For *Salop County Council*

(Mr. J. Humphreys, Haulier, Paul)

2 Ton Lime. Waggon No. *2100*

Date *25/11/190*

This Waggon must be unloaded within 48 hours after arrival, or Demurrage will be charged at the rate of 3s. per day.

Take care of this Sheet which should be carefully folded and returned in the empty Truck. *to oblige*

Please empty & return this truck at once

FROM
BLACK PARK COLLIERY,
Near RUABON.

To
LLYNCLYS.

For _____

Coal.   Wagon No. _____

Date _____

This Wagon must be unloaded within 48 hours after arrival, or Demurrage will be charged at the rate of 3s. per day.

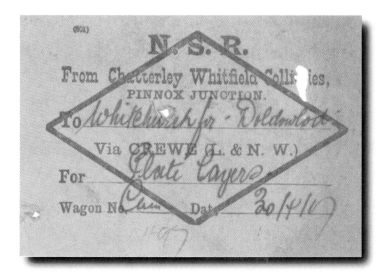

N. S. R.
From Chatterley Whitfield Collieries,
PINNOX JUNCTION.
To *Whitchurch for - Doldowlod*
Via CREWE (L. & N. W.)
For *Plate Layers*
Wagon No. *Cam*   Date *20/4/10*

Appendix I

Local Maps

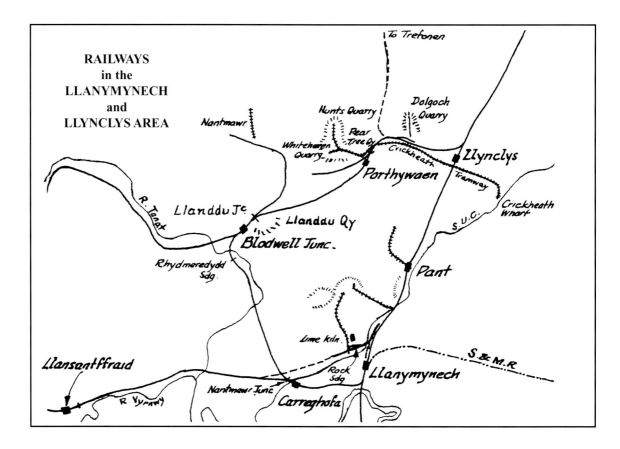

Wagon label from Porthywaen Lime Co.

48

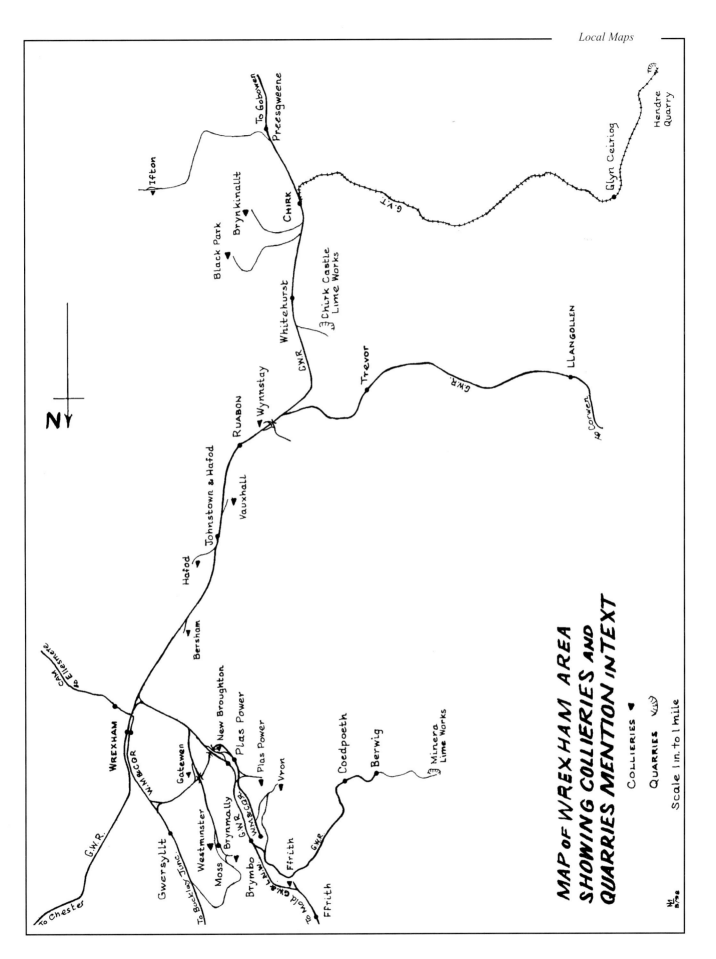

MAP of WREXHAM AREA
SHOWING COLLIERIES AND
QUARRIES MENTION IN TEXT

COLLIERIES ▼
QUARRIES 〰

Scale 1 in. to 1 mile

To Gobowen

Preesgweene

Hendre Quarry

Ifton

Brynkinallt

CHIRK

Black Park

Glyn Ceiriog

Whitehurst

Chirk Castle Lime Works

G.W.R.

GWR

Wynnstay

Trevor

LLANGOLLEN

GWR

To Corwen

RUABON

Johnstown & Hafod

Vauxhall

Hafod

Bersham

To Ellesmere

GWR

WREXHAM

WM&CQR

New Broughton

Plas Power

Plas Power

Gatewen

Vron

Coedpoeth

Berwig

Minera Lime Works

Westminster

Brynmally

GWR

WM&CQR

Ffrith

Moss

Brymbo

GWR LNW

Ffrith

To Mold

GWR

To Buckley Junc.

Gwersyllt

To Chester

N↑

49

Index of Traders on the Cambrian

Showing Wagon Owners at Cambrian Stations

Aberdovey
Evan Davies
Griffith Davies & Son
Lewis Lewis

Abermule
J Morris Jones
Parry & Son

Aberystwyth   **2**
J B Balcombe
George Green
Ellis John
J Jenkin-Jones
Peter Jones   **3**
Lisburn Mines Co. Ltd.
Charles Meehan & Son   **4**
Henry E Taylor
Thomas & Jones   **5**
William Thomas

Barmouth
John Lewis   **6**
Ellis Morris

Bow Street
T J Morgan & Sons

Bettisfield
H E Huxley

Builth Wells
Thomas Lant
BQC   **7**

Caersws
John Williams

Dinas Mawddwy
Mawddwy Coal & Lime Co.

Dyffryn
Morris Griffiths Williams

Ellesmere
Thomas Chetwood
A E Miner
E Nixon
W & W Nunnerley   *4*

Fairbourne
E Evans & Son

Four Crosses
John Davies Rogers

Llanbedr & Pensarn
Richard Bros.
Robert Richards

Llanbrynmair
Thos. Humphreys

Llandinam
Richard Griffiths

Llanfihangel
Lewis Edwards
William Morgan

Llanfyllin
Llanfyllin Coal & Lime Co.   *6*

Llanidloes
D Morgan & Son
John Godfrey Wienholt Bowen
Frank Price

Llanrhaiadr
J E Vaughan

Llanymynech
D Evans

Llynclys
Llynclys Lime Works
Montgomeryshire Coal & Lime Co.
Savin & Co.

Machynlleth
Edward Davies   **12**
Richard Evans
J Lumley & Son   **13**
R E Pugh   *14*, **14**

Minffordd
Pwllheli Granite Co.   *15*, **15**
Syenite Paving Setts Quarry Co. Ltd.

Nantmawr
R S France
Lilleshall Co.   **16**

Newtown
John Evans
D H Jones
Thomas Parry Jones
Herbert Lewis Matthews
W Morris & Sons
R Parry
Emily Catherine Schofield

Oswestry
N Davies
William Edwards
Griffiths & Jones
Hughes, Lloyd & Clare
J Huxley & Sons
William Jenkinson
W J Johnson & Son Ltd.
W Martin & Co.
T Milner   *16*
James Nurse   *17*

Oswestry (Cont.)
Oswestry Independent Co-op Society
George Rogers
E Shepherd   **17**
W H Thomas & Sons
Williams & Wilson   *18*
Jos. Williams & Son Ltd.   **18**

Penrhyndeudraeth
Williams & Jones
Evan Jones
William Morris Jones
John Roberts
J E Williams   **19**

Penybontfawr
F Ambrose

Pool Quay
T Finney & Son

Porthywaen
Porthywaen Lime Co.   *7 - 11*
Steetley Lime & Basic Co.
Steetley Lime Co.
Steetley Co. Ltd.   *2, 12, 13*, **1, 9 - 11**
John Robert Williams

Portmadoc
Robert Hughes
John Jones
Pensyflog Iron Mining Co.
Ellis Williams

Pwllheli
Eifionyd Farmers Assoc.
Evan Williams

Rhayader
Rhayader Granite Quarries Ltd.

Towyn
Lewis Edwards
John Humphries
Morris Jones & Sons
Tonfanau Granite Quarries   **20**

Welshpool
A E Breeze
Breeze Bros.
The Farmers Lime, Coal & General
                    Supply Co.
W E Morgan   **21**
J & M Morris Ltd.
John Norris
Owen & Hamer
Parry, Son & Parry
Peate Bros.   *5*

In Appendices II and III, the numbers in Italics are Figure numbers of drawings; those in Bold are Plate numbers of photographs.

Foreign Traders on the Cambrian

Showing Foreign Traders' Wagons recorded at Cambrian Stations

Aberdovey
Davies Coal & Coke Co. (Birmingham)
Joseph Hawkins & Son Ltd., Cannock Old Coppice Colliery
Ruabon Coal & Coke Co.   *25*
Richard Williams & Sons Ltd. Wagon No.423

Aberystwyth
Wynnstay Colliery

Bettisfield
J H Billington (Chester)   *19*
Mossfield Colliery Ltd.

Caersws
Ruabon Coal & Coke Co.   *25*

Doldowlod
Bargoed Coal Co. Ltd. (Abernant Colliery)
Brereton Colliery Co., near Rugeley
Chatterley-Whitfield Colliery, Pinnox Junction
James & Emanuel
Midland Coal, Coke & Iron Co. Ltd., Apedale Colliery
Old Radnor Trading Co., Dolyhir   *22 - 24*
A Thomas & Co., 29 Rutland St., Swansea (RCH 1933)
E D Williams, Hollybush Colliery   **33**

Forden
Cannock & Rugeley Colliery
North & South Wales Coal Co.

Four Crosses
Black Park Colliery   **23, 24**

Kerry
Cannock Chase Colliery Co.
Frederic Chubb   **30**

Llanfihangel
Rd. Williams & Sons, 39 Old Hall St., Liverpool

Llanfyllin
Black Park   **23, 24**
Westminster Colliery   **36**

Llangynog
Barton & Co.

Llanymynech
Florence Coal & Iron Co. Ltd.   **31**
Frederic Chubb   **30**
Glebe Colliery, Fenton   **31**
Westminster Colliery   **36**

Llynclys
Barton & Co.   **22**
Bassano Bros. Ltd., Cheadle
Black Park Colliery   **23, 24**
Brereton Collieries

Llynclys (Cont.)
Brynkinalt Colliery   **27**
Chatterley-Whitfield   **29**
Lilleshall Co. Ltd (Donnington Colliery)   **16**
Minera Lime Co.   *21,* **34**
Powell Duffryn Steam Coal Co. Ltd.
Ruabon Coal & Coke Co.   *25*
Salt Union
Sneyd Collieries
Stafford Coal & Iron Co.
H Sowter
Vauxhall Colliery Co.   **35**
Westminster Colliery   **36**

Minffordd
Broughton & Plas Power   **25, 26**

Montgomery
Cannock Chase Colliery Co.
Brereton Collieries

Oswestry
William Blake (Hereford)
Bignall Hill Colliery
Ceiriog Granite Co.   **28**
Foxfield Collieries
Shelton Iron & Coal Co.

Penmaenpool
Hanwood Colliery

Porthywaen
Brynkinalt Colliery (W Y Craig & Sons Ltd.)   **27**
Talk-o'-th'-Hill Colliery
Thomas & Co.

Portmadoc
Wigan Coal & Iron Co.

Rhayader
Cannock Chase Colliery Co.

Talyllyn (North)
Mynydd Maen Colliery, Pontypool
H Stothert & Co., Cardiff

Towyn
Foxfield Colliery Co.

Van (Branch)
Ruabon Coal & Coke Co.   *25*

Welshampton
Chatterley-Whitfield Colliery   **29**
Fenton Colliery

Bibliography and References

Including Sources consulted whilst preparing this Book

1.   Tavender, Len, *Coal Trade Wagons*
     pub L Tavender 1991.
2.   Green, C C, *Coast Lines of the Cambrian Railways*
     pub Wild Swan Publications Ltd. 1996.
3.   Green, C C, *Coast Lines of the Cambrian Railways*
     Vol 2.
3A. Green, C C, *Cambrian Railways Album* Vol 1.
     pub Ian Allan.
4.   Green, C C, *Cambrian Railways Album* Vol 2.
     pub Ian Allan 1981.
5.   Christiansen, R and Miller, R W
     The Cambrian Railways Vol.2 plate 9
     pub David & Charles 1968.
6.   Cartwright, R and Russell, R T,
     The Welshpool & Llanfair Light Railway
     pub David & Charles.
7.   Boyd, J I C, *Narrow Gauge Railways in South
     Caernarvonshire*, p34.
8.   Hughes, Stephen, *The Archaeology of the
     Montgomeryshire Canal*
     pub The Royal Commission on Ancient and Historical
     Monuments in Wales. ISBN 87 118400 2
9.   Pearce, Adrian (Ed.) *Mining in Shropshire*
     pub Shropshire Books, 1995. ISBN 0 903802 63 5
10. Lerry, G G, *Collieries of Denbighshire*
     pub Wyn Williams (Publishers) Ltd. Wrexham 1968.
11. Lerry, G G, Henry Robinson, *Pioneer of Railways
     into Wales*
     pub Woodalls Ltd., Oswestry 1949.
12. Baker, Allan C, *The Cheadle Collieries and their
     Railways*
     pub Trent Valley Publications. ISBN 0 948131 12 8
13. Baker, Allan C, *Industrial Locomotives of North
     Staffordshire*
     ISBN 0 901096 97 0
14. Johnson, Peter, *Celebration of Steam, North Wales*
     pub Ian Allen. ISBN 0 7110 2378 6
15. Cooke, R A, *Atlas of the GWR*
     pub Wild Swan Publications Ltd. ISBN 0 906867 65 7
16. Wilson, Edward, *The Ellesmere and Llangollen Canal*
     pub Phillimore & Co. 1975. ISBN 0 85033 109 9
17. Milner, W J, *The Glyn Valley Tramway*
     pub Oxford Publishing Co. 1984. ISBN 0 86093 286 9
18. Bennett, John (Ed.), *Minera. Lead Mines and Quarries*
     pub Wrexham Maelor Borough Council 1995.
     ISBN 0 952 55 29 06
19. Kelly, Philip J, *Road Vehicles of the Great Western
     Railway*
     pub Oxford Publishing Co. 1973. ISBN 902888 12 9
20. Jeuda, Basil, *The Knotty*
     pub Lightmoor Press. ISBN 1 899889 01 9

21. Bradley, V J, *Industrial Locomotives of North Wales*
     ISBN 0 901096 72 5
22. de Havilland, John, *Industrial Locomotives of Dyfed
     & Powys*
     ISBN 0 901096 84 9
23. Bridges, Alan J (Ed.), *Industrial Locomotives of
     Cheshire, Shropshire & Herefordshire*
     ISBN 901096 32 6
24. A Bodlander, A, Hamby, M, Leadbetter, H and
     Southern, D
     Oswestry Railways. A collection of Pictures
     pub Bridge Books, Wrexham. ISBN 1 872424 44 9
25. Matthews, Peter, *Private Owner Wagons*
     pub MAP 1973.
26. Essery, R J, Rowland, D P and Steel, W O
     British Goods Wagons from 1887 to the Present Day
     pub David & Charles.
27. Lewis, W J, *Born on a Perilous Rock, Aberystwyth
     Past and Present*
     pub Cambrian News (Aberystwyth) Ltd.
     ISBN 0 900439 04 1
28. Lloyd, Lewis, *Pwllheli, The Port and Mart of Llyn*
     ISBN 0 901330 89 2
29. Blick, David E, *The Old Metal Mines of Mid-Wales*
30. Lloyd, Mike, *The Tanat Valley Light Railway*
     pub Wild Swan Publications Ltd. ISBN 0 906867 92 4
31. Wren, Wilfred J, *The Tanat Valley*
     pub David & Charles (Holdings) Ltd. 1968.
32. Williams, C J, *Industry in Clwyd an illustrated history*
     pub Clwyd Record Office 1986. ISBN 0 903952 93 9
33. Cozens, Lewis, *The Mawddwy Railway*
     pub by the author 1954.
34. Hudson, Bill, *Private Owner Wagons*
     pub Oakwood Press.
35. Handbooks pub RCH 1926, 1933.
36. *Handbook of Stations* pub RCH 1938.
37. *List of Collieries* pub GWR June 1907 and 1924.
38. Proceedings Inst. Mech. Engineers 1852.
     'Construction of Railway Wagons'
39. Proceedings Inst. Mech. Engineers 1884.
     'South Wales Mineral Wagons'
40. *Modellers' BackTrack* Vol.3 No.6 Feb/Mar 1994.
41. *Railway Magazine* Oct 1903.
42. *Model Railway News*
43. *Model Railway Constructor*
44. *Model Engineer* 16th July 1908.
45. *Historical Model Railway Society Journal* No.8.
46. Cambrian Railways Modelling Circle Newsletters
47. Birmingham Library, ref. 38-59 Drg.4380.
48. Shropshire Records Unit, ref. 3966/Misc/2/32.